SPRING CLEANING

SPRING CLEANING

Jeff Campbell
and
The Clean Team

A DELL TRADE PAPERBACK

A DELL TRADE PAPERBACK
Published by
Dell Publishing
a division of
Bantam Doubleday Dell Publishing Group, Inc.
666 Fifth Avenue
New York, New York 10103

ISBN: 0-440-50162-8

Printed in the United States of America
Published simultaneously in Canada

April 1989

10 9 8 7 6 5 4 3 2 1

SEM

Dedication

As the subject is cleaning, and as that subject often involves a mother's duty, I'm often asked about the influence of my own mother, Betty Campbell, on my career choice and interest in cleaning. Actually, I don't remember. I do remember we had a dog back then, and now that I have a couple of them myself, I know how much hair is flying around my house. I've tried to remember seeing dog hairs in my childhood home but I can't. Whatever she did with them and whatever I picked up from her about this subject, "Thanks, Mom. I'm enjoying myself."

/

Acknowledgments

Bill Redican was my writing collaborator and partner in this effort. We both wrote chapters and then passed them back and forth to edit, correct, and make sensible. It's been a fun effort (practically all the time) and our friendship remains intact. Thank you.

Keith Taylor, with his special skills and dedication, kept The Clean Team cleaning and patiently helped resolve disputes about techniques and products. Thanks again.

Mike Curry, Eric Ernsberger, John Redding, and other members of The Clean Team cheerfully offered their consultation based on an expert involvement with their work.

Neal Devore, owner of Economy Sales in San Francisco, together with his great staff, shared their extensive knowledge of products and procedures with us.

Miguel Cosio, manager of the custodial staff of the City and County of San Francisco and instructor of custodial classes, shared the experience of a lifetime involved in this profession.

Frank Gromm III, of Gromm's Rug and Upholstery Cleaners, Montara, California, offered excellent advice on carpet spotting based upon his 25+ years of experience.

William B. Meyer, purveyor of fine antique silver in San Francisco, offered generous and expert advise on polishing and caring for silver.

Lorraine Umphrey, Hardsurface Products Manager of L. D. Brinkman Co., Ontario, California, was kind enough to help with information on linoleum and other resilient floor coverings.

Contents

INTRODUCTION

This is a book about housecleaning written for people who would rather be doing just about anything else. It is the second such book. The first, *Speed Cleaning* (Dell, 1987), presented The Clean Team's unique system of cleaning that relies on principles of time-and-motion economy to reduce cleaning time by half or more. Its concern was saving time during weekly cleaning—the tasks most of us regard as routine cleaning (e.g., dusting, vacuuming, and cleaning sinks and toilets).

Speed Cleaning was the first systematic approach to cleaning an entire household ever presented in print. But it also had a special emphasis: to get it over with as soon as possible—not to linger, fuss, dawdle, or dwell over it. You see, we were really writing just as much about personal freedom as we were about cleaning: how to free yourself from one of daily life's great drudgeries—housecleaning.

People all across the country understood and responded. We heard from over 10,000 of you last year alone. And one of the things you told us is that you'd also like to learn how to tackle the heavy-duty cleaning chores as well as the weekly tasks. We listened to you (*thank you!*), and the present book is the result.

For those of you not familiar with *Speed Cleaning*, we'd better explain that we're not going to offer a collection of household hints. Instead, we will teach you a system that uses solid tools instead of gadgets, generalized cleaners instead of dozens of specialized products that clutter up your home, and a step-by-step approach instead of isolated suggestions. Our emphasis is to get it over with and move on to other things. Tips, hints, and gadgets don't enable you to do the job from start to finish. At best, they are unrelated, useful ideas. At worst, they are a disappointing waste of your time and money.

Many of us, burdened with the time pressures of working, commuting, and trying to hold a household together, barely seem to have time to butter the toast in the morning, let alone strip the floors. Presuming you can find the time, *how do you start? And will there be anything left of the weekend if you do?* This book offers relief on both accounts.

Spring Cleaning addresses two major types of housecleaning:

1. **Spring cleaning:** Tasks that need to be done once or twice a year—stripping and waxing floors, cleaning windows, walls, rugs, etc.

   We will show you how to do major housecleaning tasks the smart and fast way on your first attempt. And to do them right so you won't have to repeat them for the longest possible time. Our method also makes the jobs less frustrating and more rewarding.

2. **Heavy (catch-up) cleaning.** Tasks that you have to do to be able to start routine cleaning. These include tasks you don't do every time you clean but that you can't ignore forever.

   It is for all those who, despite their best intentions, are always falling behind or just never get started. Not that we blame you. We all know what's lurking behind the refrigerator and under the sofa cushions, but we also know it's not going to go away by itself. Many households need a thorough cleaning before a rational person would even attempt weekly or maintenance cleaning. There's little point in cleaning just the top layer of crud over and over; the unexcavated layers are still there.

We are going to teach you one very good way to do each job. It's not that there aren't other alternatives. We just aren't going to mention them. Our steadfast aim is to show you how get cleaning over with so you have time to go to that evening class, or watch the football game, or take the kids to the park, or whatever else it is in your life that needs some time to flourish. We could gather everything there is to know about window washing, for example, into one surprisingly large book. It would take you all weekend to read it, let alone put it into practice. That's not what we're up to. We will give you as few decisions to make as possible about cleaning methods and products.

The flip side of this issue would be not *enough* information to do the job. We've read books on cleaning that just raise issues and never get around to telling you *what to do* or *how to do it*. After reading them we still don't know exactly where to start or what materials to use or where to find the materials.

It would be wrong to be smug about all this. We just didn't have a choice, that's all. The Clean Team is a San Francisco company that specializes in residential cleaning, working in teams of three. We clean San Francisco homes about 15,000 times a year. And we're fast too: Our teams can clean an average house in 42 minutes, or a one-bedroom apartment in about 21 minutes. No fooling.

If we didn't develop a way of cleaning houses fast we would be doing it for fun, not profit. The profit margin for residential cleaning is just too small to waste a minute's time. Every move has to count, and we also had to find the right products that wouldn't slow us down *or* make us redo our work. So we field-tested hundreds of products and innumerable strategies to cut our time to the bone. And we kept records on it all—every single visit—to make sure we were making progress and not just hoping we were. It was hard, and we learned some expensive lessons along the way. But through *Spring Cleaning* you can learn from our experience much faster.

What immediately follows is a list of The Clean Team Rules. These are the principles we've distilled after years of field experience. But there's more to cleaning than rules. In Chapter 2 we review the products that we mention in the book and that we use every day on the job. We also provide a way for you to order them for your own use (see the appendix). In the remaining chapters, we present step-by-step instructions for each of the major (and a few minor) chores, one at a time.

We recommend that you read Chapters 1 and 2 (on the rules and cleaning products) and then turn to the section that covers that project you have in mind. And remember to give yourself time to round up the materials you'll need—either from us or from local suppliers.

1 THE CLEAN TEAM RULES

The Clean Team rules are the ones we practice every business day of the year. As a business, we really don't have a choice about saving time, but you do: You can continue wasting time on an activity that you probably detest, or you can learn a systematic method to get it over with fast. (At least you have the luxury of a choice—that's something of a consolation!)

We formalized our rules after we realized that we needed a way to train new Clean Team members in as efficient a way as we worked. Our first attempt at a rational list was made after scouring the library (surprise!) for literature on the principles of time-and-motion economy.

Well, the literature's formal rules were just that—too formal. But we found that if we sat down and transcribed our practical experience directly into a set of rules, we were coming up with almost exactly the same intent as more traditional time-and-motion principles. So here they are—more tried-and-true than they may at first appear, because they have been put through the wringer (so to speak) by generations of Clean Teams in legions of homes.

1. **Make every move count.** This is probably the most important rule, so let's elaborate a bit.

    Perhaps you know what it's like to clean without a system. Let's say you are working your way around the room with the furniture polish in one hand and a polishing cloth in the other. You run into a nest of fingerprints on the woodwork. You don't want to spray polish on the wall, so you drop what you're doing, walk to the kitchen, and rummage around for a spray cleaner. It's not where it was the last time you saw it. You mutter to yourself and hurl accusations at whoever else lives in the house. You finally find it behind the bag of cat litter. The cat is eyeing you suspiciously. You traipse back across the house to the fingerprints, at which time you realize that you cannot use the polishing cloth with the liquid cleaner.

Presuming you can resist the TV on the trip to and from the kitchen to get a paper towel or two or three, you now feel ready to tackle the fingerprints. You spray. You scrub. You inspect. The smudges are still there. Just the upper layer of dirt was excavated. The bottom layer must consist of some challenging substance like raspberry jam. But by now the poor paper towel is shredding. An expedition back to the kitchen follows. The TV is looking better and better. . . .

Another common approach to cleaning is more systematic but it still wastes a lot of time. In this strategy, a person goes around the room once per task. Once to pick things up, once to dust, once to do fingerprints. Once to do the upholstery, and so forth. Trouble is, as I'm sure you're aware, every step that you take that is not engaged in that task is wasted and will have to be repeated for the next task. If you ever draw a map of your actual progress around the room it would be a genuine revelation. And if you don't do it in the right order you're in trouble too. One of our customers explained her system, in which she first vacuumed (because it seemed most important to her) and then dusted. Not such a good idea if you want the dust to go away.

You get the point. We've all been cleaning like that for years. That was our grandmother's full-time method and nobody ever taught us any differently. Add to these miseries a bad memory ("Now where did I put that rag?"), a lack of supplies ("Who used the last of the paper towels without replacing them!"), and one million distractions ("The dog ate my homework!"). *That's* where the time evaporates.

But ah! Relief is at hand. Rule 1: *Make every move count.* That means working your way around the room once—not backtracking. To accomplish this, you'll have to carry all your tools, equipment, and supplies with you. How much faster (not to mention more pleasant) it would be to have everything you need within reach—without having to take a single step. That's what a cleaning apron does. It's worth its weight in chocolate truffles. And it's at the heart of Rule 1.

If you observe this rule correctly, you will stop wasting steps that will have to be repeated. Train yourself to detect even a single step that was made without purpose or that will have to be repeated. And then just quit making those extra steps or movements. They waste time. It will become instinctive after a very short while.

No need to be neurotic about it either. It's more a matter of attention than tension. After a while, it actually becomes a pleasure to try to hone down your movements to make every one count. There's a real sense of accomplishment to it. That's how you turn a "boring" task into one that both elicits alertness and gives some measure of satisfaction. Also a certain well-earned smugness, because you know you're going to be done that much faster. We're serious about cutting your time in *half* too: We train people all the time. You can even reduce it by substantially more than half if you apply yourself.

This once-around-the-room rule is not unique to cleaning, of course. I once asked a journeyman painter why he kept a 2-inch paintbrush in the paint tray along with the roller. He explained that instead of going around the room once to do the trim and another time to roll out the walls, he worked his way around the room only once. He did the trim with the brush as far as he could safely reach. Next he set the brush in the shallow end of the tray (out of the way of the roller) and rolled out as far as he could safely reach. Then he repositioned the ladder and started the next area of the wall. That simple strategy probably saved him 30% of his time. (I wish he'd write a book called *Speed Painting!*)

It is true that when we say to work your way around the room "once," we are using poetic license just a teensy bit. Obviously you cannot drag a vacuum cleaner around with you as you dust. Likewise, we haven't yet figured out a way to mop the kitchen floor at the same time that you work your way around the kitchen cleaning the counters, refrigerator, stove, sink, and so forth.

The point is that you do, indeed, have to go around the room more than once: once to clean and once to do the floor. If there were a way to merge them both into one trip, you'd better believe we'd do it.

2. **Use the right tools.** Housecleaning, as an activity, has the unfortunate distinction of having accumulated more gadgets than tools. Maybe it's because it isn't

esteemed enough to merit the distinction of its own tools. Baloney! Anything that takes this much time *needs* it own tools. Any other task that is taken seriously has developed its own equipment, and by now you must surely know that we take housecleaning seriously.

As we said under Rule 1, the major tool in saving time is a *cleaning apron.* That's what is going to make it possible for you to move your other tools, supplies, and equipment around the room with you within arm's reach.

And what are you going to put in this apron? Well, we happen to have a few suggestions. First, you should carry with you a set of three tools adaptable enough to be useful in all sorts of circumstances and in all sorts of rooms in the house: a heroic version of a toothbrush, a single-edge razor blade in a holder, and a small scraper or putty knife. We'll describe these items in detail in the next chapter.

The rest of the stuff in the apron will be supplies (e.g., furniture polish) and equipment (e.g., cleaning cloths) needed to get the job done. Also lined pockets for debris or a wet sponge. It's that simple. But it took us four or five years to *get* it that simple—after dozens of design changes to make the apron's seven pockets and two loops work just right.

3. **Work from top to bottom.** Every once in a while some brave souls announce a breakthrough in cleaning: that centuries of common wisdom are wrong, and you should defy both common sense and gravity by working from bottom to top. Dear folks, some things are eternal. This is one of them. Work from top to bottom.

Ah! But your active mind is racing to find an exception, and it believes it has come up with a real killer—washing walls. Why? Because you have noticed that when you start at the top, dribbles of cleaning solution find their way down the wall and leave clean and annoyingly visible trails behind them. It may indeed look like you're bleaching streaks in the wall, but you're not. The dribbles are just precleaning modest little paths earthward. Nothing to worry about. Wipe them off, clean over them as you work your way down the wall, and they will eventually blend in. (More of this in Chapter 6, "Washing Walls.")

4. If it isn't dirty, don't clean it. This rule isn't as dumb as it sounds. You'd be amazed at the amount of time that is wasted cleaning surfaces that weren't dirty to begin with. When Clean Team trainees first tackle the front of a refrigerator, for example, their first impulse is to spray the whole thing head to foot with liquid cleaner. Meanwhile, the old pros size it up and spot-clean the fingerprints, polish the chrome, and move on. The result in both cases: a clean door—but with an obvious difference in time. Vertical surfaces are almost never as dirty as horizontal ones, and areas high up in a room are cleaner than lower ones. So all parts of a room don't merit equal zeal or attention.

5. Don't rinse or wipe a surface before it's clean. There you are, scrubbing away at something unspeakable on the kitchen counter and wishing you were done. You decide that *surely* all the grunge is gone by now and you take a chance on rinsing. Alas, the grunge remaineth. But you secretly knew it was still there all along, didn't you? You were just trying to wish it away. Nice try, but grunge cannot read your mind. And now you endure the time-consuming task of starting all over again.

 The alternative to this little game? Learn to "see through" the dirt you're cleaning until you're really done, so you only have to rinse or wipe once. Actually, you're often "feeling through," not seeing. That is, keep scrubbing until you feel the actual surface below the dirt—a real change in the way the brush touches the surface. And try to disengage your capacity for wishful thinking at the same time, which is more difficult. There's no hurry to wipe off the gooey mess that you're making. Just bide your time until the area you're working on is really clean all the way to the surface. The scrub brush or cloth will feel different as soon as the grunge is really gone. *Then* wipe clean. You will be thrilled with your new self-discipline, but it is one of those quiet little joys that cannot easily be shared.

6. Don't keep working after it's clean. (Or "Enough! Enough already!") To be sure, this rule is abused far less often than the previous rule. It's just that sometimes we

have a need to keep scrubbing in an utterly useless manner. The point is simple: If you're paying attention to what you're doing, you're going to detect when you've hit ground zero more quickly. Then just stop, wipe or rinse clean, and move on.

7. **If what you're doing isn't going to work, shift to a more heavy-duty cleaner or tool.** Most of the time, we do this instinctively. If you're cleaning the stove top and come upon a little glob that doesn't easily wipe up with a cloth, your impulse would be to take after it with a more heavy-duty tool: your fingernail. We'll offer some better options—like a toothbrush, scraper, razor blade, or white pad. But the idea is to use as little cleaning power as possible to save the most time. Then shift to the next heaviest tool when necessary.

   You'll finish fastest by shifting tools or cleaners as early as possible in the cleaning process. Red Juice (explained in the next chapter) is going to work a lot better and faster on fingerprints than is Blue Juice (ditto). A lot of this will be learned by experience, of course, but it is also one of the reasons we wrote *Spring Cleaning*—to pass along some of our experience so you can be spared all the hard work we went through.

8. **Keep your tools in impeccable shape.** Store your cleaning supplies coherently and always in the same place—not stashed in some dark cubbyhole where you will have to rummage through everything to find what you're looking for. If you have the room, store your supplies in a closet. If you have to use the area under the sink, consider installing shelves to keep things organized. Cleaning trays with separate compartments can also be a great help. You can reach in and pull out what you need quickly, and you can also have a separate tray for each of the major types of household cleaning: kitchen, bathroom, and dusting. If you're zeroing in on the bathroom, for example, you'd just grab the bathroom tray and you'd be on your way.

   If you let your razor get rusty it will cause more havoc than cleaning. If you wash your furniture-polishing cloth along with a rag that was just used with abrasive cleaner, your polishing cloths may pick up some of the grit and start scratching your furniture. If you ignore the funny whine your vacuum is making, it just may burn out a motor or break a fan belt to get your attention. If you store your mop in a damp spot you may have to send it to the Pasteur Institute to subdue the mold population.

9. **Repetition makes for smoother moves.** No motor skill that we are aware of comes without practice—good old repetition. To make repetition work smoothly, you've got to put your tools back in the same place every time—both in your apron and in the cleaning tray. When you reach for your Red Juice you don't have time to look to see if: (a) it is really there, or (b) it is another kind of cleaner. So it's important that the Red Juice is *always* on the same apron loop time after time. Once you get your cleaning routine down, don't mess with it unless you have a compelling reason.

10. **Pay attention.** One of the mottoes of the Jesuit Order of Catholics is *Age quod agis*—"Do what you are doing." Zen Buddhists call the same idea "mindfulness." If what you're doing is cleaning, then just clean— that's all. Anything that Jesuits and Buddhists independently discover is worth serious scrutiny.

If you work with full attention, you are working at the edge of your full abilities— one of the reasons that video games are so addictive. Working at the edge of your full abilities in *fun*. In spite of yourself. Besides, you'll get the task over with quicker, and you'll probably do a better job of it. All by not working harder, just smarter—by working at full attention. Pay attention to the work that you're doing right in front of you. Just clean.

11. **Keep track of your time.** It's helpful to feel encouraged about what you're doing, and the only way to do that is to keep track of your progress. A healthy dose of discouragement isn't such a bad idea either, as long as you have some idea of what's contributing to the lack of progress and then take steps to correct it.

12. Use both hands. Why not, if you are so blessed? Using only one is like typing with one hand.

One reader called our attention to the fact that not all folks have two hands. We did not mean to be insensitive—it's just that we wanted to point out that you should use all of your available resources and not leave any such capacity idle. If you are blessed with two hands, reach for the polishing cloth with one hand as the other one sprays furniture polish. Clean with one hand while the other one stabilizes an object. One hand can scrub with a brush while the other manages the cleaning cloth to wipe up. The examples are endless.

13. If there are more than one of you, work as a team. Working in a team has lots of advantages. Foremost among them, from our point of view, is that you get done sooner! Besides, maybe someone else helped get the house dirty to begin with.

Disputes over household chores are ranked as one of the most important sources of household disharmony. Andy Rooney recently questioned a statistic he had read claiming that 63% of all households argue about housework. He thought it was more like 100%. We agree. Learning to work together on these chores may get you back not only your spare time. Who knows, peace may break out in your home.

And for husbands who have felt frozen out of the household scene, working on a team with the rest of your family can be the way out. We believe many men have stayed away from cleaning because they haven't been taught a step-by-step, systematic approach—as they have for carpentry or mechanics—and they have developed a scorn for it. In that light, it's easier to see how men in our culture developed an aversion to cleaning. But there's no reason for that attitude to continue now. And many wives are also working 40 hours a week and commuting. We're on everybody's side—men or women or children—who want to learn a systematic approach to this work. The floor doesn't know who's mopping it!

Those are the rules we distilled from literally years spent cleaning houses—nearly 100,000 times. Read them over once or twice, and you'll find them seeping into your way of working. You'll also be discovering them on your own as you develop the satisfaction of working in a way that uses your time and abilities at maximum efficiency.

But you need more than rules. Rules are the *why* of all this. You also need to know *how* to put the rules into play. And *what* to use in order to do it. That's what the following chapters will do. First we'll review the cleaning tools, equipment, and supplies that will get you out of the house fastest. Then we'll go step by step through the heavy cleaning tasks that you are likely to encounter in your home.

2 TOOLS, EQUIPMENT, AND SUPPLIES

As you know, there are a lot of cleaning products on the market. Accordingly, there are a lot of choices to make. How do you know which ones work? Are there any real differences among products? Should you believe the ads? Should you keep using what your mother did 15 years ago?

One of the first things we realized when getting our cleaning business off the ground was that we were going to have to wade through that array of products and make some decisions about which ones worked and which ones didn't. We learned quickly that there were significant differences between products that appeared to be similar. And many are quite expensive, which makes the comparison process one that cannot be taken too lightly.

And we also learned that several products that were as traditional as Mom and apple pie were just too slow. An example in this regard is the sponge. A sponge doesn't scrub, rinse, or even absorb as well as plain old cotton cleaning cloths. As a result, sponges tend to leave streaks behind—which means extra work and extra time.

Traditional cleaners can also be downright user-hostile. The old standby spray-on cleaners sold in grocery stores are a prime example. Some are just plain nasty when inhaled, especially in close quarters. Maybe the manufacturers (or public relations firms) think people have to hack and wheeze when using a product to believe it really works—who knows? Most also generate unwanted suds that may make you feel good, but they really slow you down because you have to get rid of the suds along with the dirt.

We began our long (in fact, continuing) search for products that are *fast* and that *work* without compromising quality. Using a product day after day, as we do, gave us an intimate knowledge of it that can be gotten in no other way. That's nothing new—just ask a skateboarder about his or her board and you will probably hear a dissertation on it molecule by molecule. Before we settled on 100% cotton restaurant table napkins as cleaning cloths, we used to buy assorted lots of rags. But the teams quickly developed a decided preference for white cotton rags—by trial and error— because they worked so much better. Before going off to work in the morning, the teams used to pick through the pile of rags with the visual acuity of bald eagles to find the white cotton ones. The tiniest bit of polyester or color doomed the cloth to the bottom of the heap. The lesson was learned.

Experience was and is our teacher, and we are passing along the benefits of it to you. Even without the right products, you're still going to save time if you learn our methods. It's just that you won't save as much. And when you get expert at anything, you just can't stand using products that get in your way—whether it's a lousy fishing pole or an ineffective furniture polish.

What follows is an alphabetical list of the products we use. One of them (the cleaning apron) is our own design. Some are plain old garden-variety cleaning products, but they're the best of their kind if you're going to save time. Others are commercial products not sold in grocery stores. And when a retail product really does what it promises to do, we don't hesitate to recommend it.

Where a product has a brand name, we're not afraid to tell you. None of their manufacturers solicited our endorsement. We're only reporting what we've learned by trying innumerable products side by side.

For any number of reasons, leisure time for most of us is finite and valuable. Maximizing that time may require trading money for time. Consider the lowly vacuum. Few of us would feel we ought to save money by cleaning with a $5 broom rather than a much more costly vacuum. But what about a professional squeegee for $10 or a wet/dry vacuum for $150? We believe that the same principle applies. If you get back your weekends, it's worth every penny.

We recognize that our method works best when you have access to the same products that we use. (There are two aspects to this system: methods and products.) Accordingly, you can order just about everything we mention—including professional formulas—through our mail-order catalog (see p. 190). At the same time, our system isn't so specific that you must use these very products. That wouldn't be fair. So we

also present complete descriptions so you can substitute other products at your discretion.

This chapter has as exhaustive a list as we could make because we had in mind all of the potential spring-cleaning chores. Obviously, if you are not contemplating cleaning the windows you will have little need for a window squeegee (unless you want to keep one handy for the glass shower door—but that's another story). Near the beginning of each chapter, we list the specific tools, supplies, and equipment that are needed for the job at hand. Certain items appear in almost all lists, such as the cleaning apron and its tools. Others are highly specific to the job.

Acrylic floor finish. It may be easier to say "acrylic wax," but it really isn't a wax. It's more like liquid plastic. Accordingly, it is not something you would want to put on wood floors (*that's* what you want liquid wax for). Acrylic finish is suitable for resilient flooring like sheet vinyl. We use a professional formula, called Acrylic High-Gloss Floor Finish, which is detergent-resistant and can be buffed to a high shine. To maintain it, it should just be swept and damp-mopped. The idea is to keep as thin a layer as possible on the floor to avoid yellowing and stripping.

Ammonia. We use clear ammonia only. There is no need whatsoever for suds to help convince you that what you're doing is working. They just get in the way. Ammonia is one of the fundamental cleaning agents. It's found in all sorts of cleaners—like brass polish, wax stripper, and glass cleaner.

Apron. The first time we cleaned a house, we showed up at the door with grocery bags full of cleaning products. (We've come a long way, baby.) It soon became crystal clear that dozens of trips back and forth to these bags for supplies was not going to cut the mustard. We had to carry around what we needed as we cleaned. After a certain amount of head-scratching, we designed our first cleaning apron.

When's the last time you saw carpenters work without an apron? Do you think they're going to run up and down a ladder every time they need another nail?

Telephone linemen have more stuff hanging off their tool belt than a Christmas tree does. Isn't it about time such a basic idea was applied to something that *you're* doing so many days of your life? We sure think so, and we've developed the first commercially available cleaning apron that we're aware of.

Over a period of years, we've fidgeted with the position of every pocket and every loop, how many of each pocket there are going to be, what size they're going to be, and how to keep the loops open so you can hang the handle of the spray bottles with ease. If any of these variables are off, the apron will be uncomfortable and less efficient.

Yeah, yeah. We've heard all the arguments. There were yowls of protest from the teams when we first introduced them: "Men do not wear aprons." (What are carpenters—sissies?) "It feels awkward." (Get over it.) "It gets in the way." (Well, yes, it does, at first. Then it doesn't. Life's like tha..) "Things will fall out." (No, they won't, if you stay awake.) "It will scare the cat." (Let the cat outside.) "The neighbors will laugh." (Wave to them as you drive away to the beach and they're still cleaning.)

Just wait. If you give it a fighting chance, you'll soon feel lost without it and you'll even have temper tantrums if someone messes with it or walks off with it.

We haven't seen or heard about a store-bought apron that works as a substitute. They range from a frilly full-length production to a leather carpenter's apron, with a few styles in between. Ours has three pockets for tools stitched just a little oversize, so the pockets keep tools standing up straight but don't restrict them from being popped in and out quickly. One of the large pockets is lined with a thick plastic bag and is used to store debris collected as you work your way around the room. The bag is held in place with simple clips for each removal and replacement. If you're working with damp rags or scrub pads, you can also line another pocket with a second plastic bag.

The apron material shouldn't be stiff enough to interfere with bending over. It must be machine-washable. It must also have loops at both sides that will stay open so you can hang spray cleaners from them smoothly.

Bleach (in a spray bottle). Use primarily to kill mold and mildew in the bathroom. If it's available in your area, we recommend Clorox Fresh Scent because it has a far less disagreeable odor than standard bleach. It's important to keep bleach stored in an opaque bottle. If light gets through to it, it can turn the product black. Also, as you must know, bleach must be treated as though it were radioactive. It will obliterate the color of almost anything—including some types of floor tile. It can even eat through stainless-steel pots if left in place long enough. (Don't ask. That was a memorable experience.)

We use Clorox either full strength or half strength diluted with water, depending on the severity of the mold population and the durability of the surface. Hospitals use bleach diluted even more as a disinfectant, so it is a very effective product. Naturally, you must be diligent not to breathe in its fumes. We usually do a spray-and-run operation in a bathroom, closing the door behind us and keeping a window open. Rinse a surface well after bleach has done its job so it doesn't go to work on the surface itself or doesn't react with any chemicals subsequently applied to the same surface.

Blue Juice (in a spray bottle). A lighter-duty liquid spray cleaner. It is intended mainly for cleaning glass, and it evaporates slightly faster than Red Juice (see p. 19) for that reason. We use a professional formula called The Clean Team Blue Juice. Like many similar retail products, it's blue—hence the name. We keep Blue Juice in a spray bottle with a blue top, as you might have guessed. Like Red Juice, it is always kept on the same apron loop.

Cleaning cloths. Besides the apron, good cleaning cloths are the next best way to cut your cleaning time down. Somewhere we've read that contemporary homemakers actually spend *more* time than our grandparents taking care of the house. One of the reasons is that we've become accustomed to modern gadgetry that occasionally is less efficient than its predecessor. The feather duster is one example of a more efficient item that's often been replaced needlessly. Cleaning cloths are another.

They're more practical than sponges for several reasons: You can scrub with them, they rinse much faster, they often absorb liquids faster, and they last much longer.

There is only one acceptable type of cleaning cloth: 100% cotton. White. Hemmed. Period. No polyester. No colored cloth, especially *red*! Red dye will wipe off onto surfaces in front of your very eyes. (Do you want to hear the horror story about the owner of a Nob Hill mansion who cleaned her white walls with red rags? No, you don't.)

After considerable research with the alternatives, we settled upon white table napkins. They're just the right size, they're hemmed, they're white, and they're usually 100% cotton. They're also expensive, but they'll last for *years* under reasonable household use. So in the long run they're actually cost-effective.

Here are a few simple diagrams on the proper folding of your cleaning cloths. Why are we bothering to delve into something so mundane? For starters, we don't want you to wad up the cloths into nasty piles and mush them into the carryall tray. When you reach for one later on, a whole bunch of them will leap out of the tray. Besides, all you will have is an unruly mass of wrinkles that will need managing before you can proceed. In addition, if you fold them properly and line them up in the carryall tray, you will have an exact idea of how many cloths you have left. And you will be very pleased with yourself.

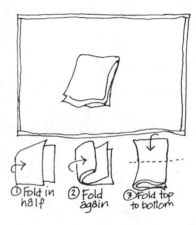

① Fold in half ② Fold again ③ Fold top to bottom

The next best alternative to table napkins are 100% cotton unfolded diapers (with hems, if possible). Salesclerks will give you strained, pitying looks when you ask for them in stores because throwaway diapers have dominated the market for several years. But if you have trouble locating a retail supply, we understand that the Sears mail-order catalog still carries them. Don't get the prefolded kind.

The third alternative is paper towels. Some people do not appreciate the inconvenience of washing the cleaning cloths, or may prefer paper towels for other reasons. If you want to use them, get the best. No point in saving 40 cents only to have the paper towel shred and leave lint everywhere. Our vote is for Bounty Microwave paper towels.

Cleaning tray. It makes good sense to keep your supplies organized between uses, so we recommend a carryall tray with steep sides (so things won't fall out) and separate compartments. If you're going to get the job over with in a hurry, you can't afford to root around in the dark under the sink for 20 minutes looking for supplies. It also makes it easy to transport supplies to the site of a major cleaning operation.

Double bucket. The perfect bucket for cleaning windows. You can keep supplies in one side and the washing solution in the other. It can also be put to splendid use on floors by having the washing or stripping solution in one side and the rinsing solution in the other.

cord and caddy

50-foot extension cord on a cord caddy. Every time you run out of cord while vacuuming you have to walk back across the house, pull the plug, mutter to yourself, find another plug, walk back to the vacuum, and wonder if you're going to make it to the end of the hall without doing it all over again. Besides being exasperating, this is a glorious waste of time. The solution is simple: a long extension cord that you plug in once only. We use a round cord because it generates fewer knots then flat cord, and if there are knots they are easier to unravel. One fine rip-snorter of a knot can take as long to unravel as it takes to vacuum a whole room, so avoid them at all reasonable costs. Instead of allowing the cord to degenerate into a nest in between uses, we wrap it around a portable rack or caddy. And when we get to work, we unravel only as much cord as we expect to use for that job.

Floor scrub brush. You know that annoying feeling when you watch the sponge mop gliiiide over dead raisins or unidentified but nevertheless sticky globs on the floor? And then it just gliiiides over them again . . . and again . . . and again? Or have you noticed how the mop manages merely to shuffle the dirt into the cracks or the grout or the fake grout? What you need is a giant version of the toothbrush. What the toothbrush is to countertops, this brush is to floors. It slides into the end of our mop after the sponge mop is removed, or else it just screws into the end of a standard threaded broom handle. It enables you to power-scrub the floor and cut time to shreds. Whatever brush you use—be it ours or one you already have at home—it should have tough, stubby, thick bristles set in a sturdy base so you can apply pressure when needed.

Furniture feeder. A suspension of carnauba wax and restorative agents in a solvent base. An application or two of furniture feeder and you'll swear you just revarnished your neglected possessions. It removes dirt, grime, oil, cooking vapors, and that nasty wax buildup, leaving a warm sheen of fine carnauba wax.

Green scrub pad/sponge ("green pad"). This is the heavy artillery in the war on dirt. It will scratch anything that moves or doesn't move if you're not careful. Think of it as green sandpaper attached to a sponge. *Always* use on a wet surface with appropriate pressure. The only consistent use we have for this is for cleaning ovens.

Kleenfast pad. Also known as a "doodle bug," this is a swiveling scrub-pad holder that can be used either with a long handle or held by hand. Scrub pads of various coarseness are available, depending on the application—e.g., scrubbing or stripping floors. The swiveling action lets you scrub floors or baseboards at a convenient angle without straining your back.

Liquid floor wax. Unless you have days to spend on the project or a host of servants at your command, paste waxing of wood floors is out of the question. The next best option, in the real world, is to spread as thin a layer as humanly possible of a liquid floor wax. It should be able to be buffed if you so wish. The formula we use is called Fortified Floor Wax.

Miscellaneous. Keep a small emergency kit at hand. Or at least know where the following are: pliers, a Phillips screwdriver, a slotted screwdriver, the telephone number to call in a medical emergency, and a spare fan belt and bag for the vacuum. We presume you already know where the bandages are.

Mop. We clean bathroom floors with cleaning cloths, but there's no escaping a mop for kitchen floors or for washing ceilings and walls. We use a serious mop made by Continental Manufacturing Company with a 13-inch sponge mop head, steel handle, and handle-operated wringer. When a piece of equipment is this large, it's got to be able to do multiple functions. (That principle is important enough to turn it into another Clean Team Rule.) In this case, we happened upon a bit of manufacturing genius that enables the mop to swap its sponge-mop head for a scrub brush *or* floor squeegee.

No-rinse stripper. Now that you've found such good floor finishes, how are you going to get the old yellow stuff off the floor, you ask? Liquid strippers are notoriously ineffective, as we're sure you will agree if you've ever tried one. But chemistry has taken a few giant strides in this regard in recent years. It had to. Many of the older floor strippers were designed more for waxes in the strict sense than for acrylics or the new "metal interlock" finishes.

But relief is at hand on two fronts: relief from the frustration of having to excavate layer after layer of old finish only to have it seem like each stripping attempt has done no good whatsoever; and relief from the fumes of many ammonia-based strippers.

This particular relief takes the form of another professional-formula wax stripper that is applied with a mop and doesn't even have to be rinsed off. Ours is called Mop-on No-Rinse Acrylic Stripper. If you prefer to use a standard floor stripper you'll still end up at the same place; you'll just have to hang in there longer and use substantially more elbow grease.

No-wax finish. For "no-wax" floors only. We recently switched to Brite—a retail product from Johnson Wax Co. It cleans and maintains a shine without building up over time, which most other products seem inevitably to do.

Oven cleaner. We haven't found a better product than Easy-Off spray.

Powdered cleanser. We use Comet.

Pumice stick. A chunk of pure lava. It's really remarkable how fast it removes scale, rust, and mineral deposits from porcelain. Just rub gently and it's gone! Other applications are limited only by the imagination: quickly cleans ovens; removes carbon buildup on grills and iron cookware; removes paint and graffiti from tile, concrete, and masonry walls; removes scale from swimming pools.

Pump-up pressure sprayer: This is a device that lets you manually pressurize a spray bottle for easy application of a liquid to a large area. Prevents wear and tear on your hand on big jobs like spraying a carpet.

Razor-blade holder. For even more heavy-duty cleaning and for specialized tasks, it's time to call on a safety razor in a holder. It's great for soap scum on shower doors, paint splatters on glass, and baked-on food on oven windows and surfaces of appliances. This is one of the three tools carried in the apron at all times.

Red Juice (in a spray bottle). A heavy-duty liquid spray cleaner. This product, along with the cleaning apron, is at the core of time saving in our system. You need a spray cleaner that you can rely on without being caustic to two- and four-footed creatures or harmful to surfaces. Ours is a professional formula called The Clean Team Red Juice.

We call it Red Juice because it's tedious to say "Please pass the heavy-duty red liquid spray cleaner." It was shortened to "Gimme some Red Juice" early in The Clean Team's history, and the shorthand stuck.

This is the finest heavy-duty cleaner/degreaser we've ever found—and we've tried them all, believe me. It's odorless, biodegradable, and safe to use around food. In its most concentrated form, it's used to degrease diesel engines, so you can imagine what it does to household dirt.

We keep Red Juice in a spray bottle with a red top so it can be identified in a flash. (When you get expert at all this, you don't even want a second's hesitation when you're looking for a cleaning product.) And we always hang it on the same side of the apron when not in use. We recommend the right side if you're right-handed (and vice versa) because you will use Red Juice more often than Blue Juice—its lighter-duty cousin.

Rubber gloves. Essential for cleaning the oven or for anything that may endanger your skin or that is too gross for words.

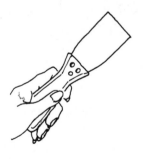

Scraper. Occasionally you will encounter mysterious globs that are difficult to remove with the toothbrush—like petrified lumps of pancake batter or squished raisins. They can be removed in seconds with a scraper. Also, there are times when the space you're cleaning is too narrow even for the toothbrush—like between the two shower doors. Those are the times to reach for this scraper. We use a 1½-inch-wide steel spatula with a plastic handle. This is one of the three tools carried in the apron at all times.

Spray bottles. We use three refillable color-coded spray bottles: one for Red Juice (red), one for Blue Juice (blue), and one for bleach (white). You need a bottle with a long and durable handle that can hook easily on the apron loops.

The spray bottle should also have a nozzle that can screw off for cleaning. The fastest way to clean a clogged nozzle is to unscrew it and scrub it with the toothbrush under running water. It's not a good idea to poke anything metallic (e.g., a needle) into the orifice because it has a good chance of deforming it and ruining the spray pattern. In many cases, what's thought to be a clogged nozzle is actually a clogged filter screen at the intake end of the tube—provided your spray bottle has one, which it should. Again, the solution is to remove the screen and scrub it under running water.

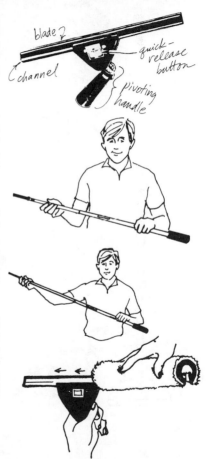

Squeegee. There's only one way to clean a window fast, and that's with a professional-quality window squeegee. We're not talking about those clumsy things with ¼-inch-thick blades that leave streaks for miles. You're far better off with a quality product that can keep a firm, flat grip on the window surface. You can choose almost any size from 6 to 22 inches, depending on the size of the windows in your house. We use the model manufactured by Ettore.

Squeegee extension pole. If you have windows that are beyond comfortable reach, we recommend a telescoping metal extension pole for the window squeegee. It saves all that time setting up the ladder, climbing up and down, worrying about falling off, and so forth. It also earns its keep as an extension pole for paint rollers and as a handle for the floor scrub brush, pushbrooms, and anything similar that has a standard threaded socket. We use the model manufactured by Ettore.

Squeegee scrub sleeve. And how do professionals *scrub* windows that are out of reach? The most practical solution is a fuzzy brush that quickly slips over the squeegee blade. With it you can transport liquid cleaning solution to the window and scrub the surface at the same time. Then it pops off quickly, and you are ready to squeegee the surface clean and dry. Actually, it's so convenient that we also recommend it for windows that are within easy reach too. We use the model manufactured by Ettore.

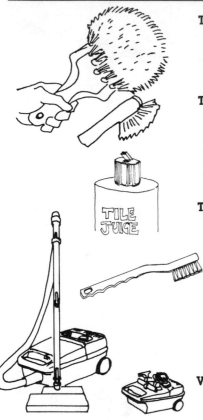

Tile brush. We found that the fastest way to spread tile juice (see below) around, as well as to scrub tile and grout at the same time, is with a large brush. It will power-scrub those shower stalls in nothing flat. We use a brush originally designed to clean commercial dairies. It has long stiff bristles, angled so they dig into difficult corners and remote recesses and rinse very quickly.

Tile Juice (in a squirt bottle). Soap scum and minerals conspire with each other to form a film that is highly resistant to cleaning, as anyone who has cleaned a shower stall can testify. You need a cleaning agent that can break up this unholy alliance, and that's what we call Tile Juice. Most such products consist of one or more acids that dissolve away the alkali soap/mineral conspiracy, and they differ mainly in their dilution. We use an industrial-strength tile cleaner. A variety of retail products are also available in grocery or hardware stores.

Toothbrush. This small brush is indispensable for getting into tight spots and even not-so-tight spots. Brushes scrub many times faster than a sponge, rag, or paper towel, and their bristles can dig into irregular surfaces as well. You'll be amazed how often a spot will not respond to wiping but will come right up when agitated with a brush and a cleaning agent like Red Juice. Unexcelled for treating carpet spots: Spray on Red Juice, agitate with brush, and blot up residue. Also used around faucet handles, on tile grout, around light switches, in shower-door runners, and so forth. Keep one in the glove compartment of your car. It will get a real workout when the car is washed.

The brush we use has bristles that are considerably thicker and stiffer than a real toothbrush's. It's a simple brush, but it's amazingly effective and took us a heck of a long time to find. This is one of the three tools carried in the apron at all times.

Vacuum cleaner (the "Big Vac"). We use a canister vacuum with two motors: one for suction and one to turn the brush in the suction head. This style is a hybrid between the traditional *upright* (the one with the big bag), whose main asset was its ability to brush up deeply lodged dirt; and the *standard canister* (the one with a hose), whose main asset was strong suction. The modified canister is an ideal combination of the best of both types.

Most vacuums offer you a choice of cloth or paper bags. After using cloth for a considerable time, we got tired of the fuss and occasional dust storms occasioned by thrashing around with cloth bags. At the same time, we found that paper bags make better suction possible. Cloth bags can clog relatively easily, and when that happens, the suction diminishes sharply. For example, one of our clients had a carpeted floor that was plagued with a recurrent layer of fine brick powder. (The bricks in the building were so old they were disintegrating.) A recently emptied cloth bag would clog within *moments* of starting to vacuum. The small grains just fill in the holes in the weave of the cloth, and the vacuum is useless. We switched to paper bags and had no further trouble.

Vacuum cleaner (the "Little Vac"). There are times when you'll need more than one vacuum if you are working in a team. And there are some tasks that are accomplished faster with a more maneuverable vacuum. So we also use this smaller canister vacuum.

Wax applicator. One of the most important things to do when waxing a floor is to apply as thin and as even a coat as possible. While you're at it, you will probably prefer not to be on your hands and knees (especially if you've just stripped the floor). The solution is one of those cheap, fake lamb's-wool wax applicators at the end of a non-backbreaking pole. When you're done with the pad, clean it or just throw it away to avoid the possibility of cross-contaminating the wax next time you use it.

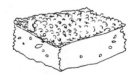

White scrub pad/sponge ("white pad"). Occasionally you must abandon brushes for the more concentrated abilities of a white scrubbing pad. White pads are the least abrasive of the several types on the market—green and gray (or black), increasingly in that order, being abrasive. White pads are widely advertised as not being likely to scratch surfaces, which is generally true. But after a while you will discover (if you haven't already) that anything can scratch anything. Or at least it seems that way. But given moderate pressure and a wet cleaning surface, your chances of scratching something with a white scrub pad are minimal. We use the one made by Scotch-Brite, which has a sponge on the other side. As much as we have reviled sponges, in this case they do serve a purpose by retaining a bit of liquid that's helpful in the scrubbing process.

3 SAFETY

We don't want to throw cold water on your efforts to master faster cleaning techniques, but it would be silly for us not to pass on some of the safety lessons we have learned along the way. You'll be concentrating, you'll be trying to pick up speed, and you'll be learning new practices and procedures—all of which can set the stage for an accident. Having said all that, you should know that cleaning is still a very safe activity. It's just nice to keep it that way—that's all.

- Don't back up without knowing who or what's behind you. Get in the habit of looking over your shoulder while you're standing still—then back up. Accidents happen when you start backing up before you check. So make it second nature to look before you move—a little like checking to see if you have your door keys before you close the front door of your house behind you.

- Don't bend over in front of a door. If it can swing toward you, someone could open it and knock you on the head with the door. If it can swing away from you, it doesn't mean it's safe. Someone could still walk through the doorway and run into you. If you must bend over in the vicinity of a door, stand off to one side. Or keep your hand on the doorknob, or block it with your foot so the door won't open, or just lock it.

- Be especially careful when you're looking up as you're working—for example, when foraging for spiderwebs on the ceiling. It's easy to get absorbed with what you're doing and walk smack-dab into something or someone. As in the case of backing up, stand still while you're cleaning and check where you're going before you take the next step. After a while you'll develop "eyes" not only in the back of your head but in your shins too (and qualify for a cameo role in *Star Trek* perhaps).

- If you drop something made of glass, get out of the way. Neither a $5 fishbowl nor a $500 vase are worth getting cut by shards of glass. The first impulse is to grab at the falling object, but that can prove to be disastrous. Let it go.

- Be careful when reaching under sofa and chair cushions with your hands. The nerve endings in your fingers make it amazingly painful to discover pins, thumb-tacks, and razor blades by touch. Likewise, be careful when you reach into your apron trash pocket with your hand. It's best not to store dangerous objects there, such as broken glass, pins, etc. Go right to a trash can with them or wrap them in other debris (such as a piece of paper) before depositing them in the apron pocket.

- Don't play Spider-Man when washing windows. Clean windows are not worth getting yourself killed for. Do not hang out of windows while supporting your weight with one hand. While working on ladders do not reach beyond the center of gravity and do not step on the upper two ladder rungs.

- When cleaning tubs that have a buildup of soap scum, remember that this soap is going to be set loose when you wash the tub *or* shower walls. As soap (unlike detergent) consists largely of fats, it is going to be slippery. So use sensible precautions to prevent slipping in the tub: Stand outside when you can. Keep your tennis shoes on if you must step inside, and step on a layer of rags when possible to give you better footing.

- Is there anyone in the world who has not been told to avoid mixing ammonia and chlorine bleach? It's simple chemistry: Ammonia releases chlorine gas from the liquid bleach, and chlorine gas is deadly.

  There are sneaky ways of mixing the two chemicals that you might not be aware of. Perhaps someone else had used ammonia on a surface and didn't rinse it off well enough. If you come along afterward and apply bleach, you may be in trouble. At the first sign of a really nasty chlorine smell, get fresh air fast. A smart idea is simply not to use ammonia in the bathroom at all. Most of the time, bleach and other cleaning products take care of the demands of bathroom cleaning, so there's no compelling reason even to take a chance of mixing ammonia and bleach. Another good reason to keep ammonia out of the bathroom is that many automatic bowl-cleaning products contain chlorine, and it would be easy to mix the two without realizing the hazard.

- Be very careful when spraying liquid cleaners in a confined area. We're sure you've noticed by now that more than one retail product on grocery shelves is murder on your lungs. Ammonia can also be a serious problem if you inhale its fumes for a prolonged period. Keep a window open when using any strong-smelling cleaner and turn on the fan. Take a fresh-air break every now and again. You're not being a wuss.

- Wear rubber gloves at the slightest provocation. Your skin is worth it. If you find yourself debating about whether you should or not, it's already time to put them on.

- Hang pictures and mirrors with decent heavy-duty hangers, nails, or screws. It's amazing how many people hang such things with thumbtacks or pushpins, in flagrant defiance of gravity. There are many more sensible things to challenge than gravity. It's right up there with death and taxes. This really does have to do with cleaning because you will have to clean these hanging items every once in a while without them falling off the wall.

- Don't clean when you're angry. Go punch a pillow (it really does work) or do a few pushups or take a few deep breaths—whatever you need to do. When you break something while cleaning, it's remarkable how often you will find that you were angry at the time. ("Next time that shameless hussy shows up in her fake furs and press-on nails I'll . . ." CRASH!) Objects just seem to fly out of hands when you're thinking nasty thoughts about shameless hussies or your boss or the IRS or the transcendent unfairness of life in general.

4   WASHING WINDOWS

If you want to improve the appearance of an entire room in one fell swoop, *wash the windows*. Few things affect how you feel about a room more than the quality of light coming in through the windows. After they're clean, it's amazing how much happier you'll feel about the room and even life in general. And once you learn how, it's also easy to do.

Excuses, Excuses

Cleaning windows has gotten a bad rap for a number of undeserving—and a few deserving—reasons. We suspect that many people don't like to do windows because they don't know how. It's hard work the way most people go about it. It makes your hands and arms hurt. It makes you sweat. It makes you break things. It makes you swear and kick the dog. And after all that grief, the streaks are often still there. Chances are you're just doing it wrong. Or maybe you've never even tried it. You've heard all the I-don't-do-windows jokes. There must be a reason for them, right? Well, maybe the reasons are wrong.

A Better Way

The good news is that it's not at all as hard as it looks. What you need most is to throw away your old newspapers and to discard exotic schemes for window cleaning that you may have learned. In their place, learn how to use a squeegee and you'll be done with window cleaning in half the time or less. And it won't be as tiring. And the windows will be cleaner. And there won't be shreds of newspaper all over the house and newsprint all over your hands.

Ever notice that you've never seen a professional window washer use Blue Juice in a spray bottle and a cloth? That's because *none* of them do. They use squeegees because squeegees work better. If you've ever stopped to watch pros at work, you've noticed how easy they make it look and how fast they finish one window and move on to the next. They aren't hot and sweaty. They can look downright comfortable. They look that way and accomplish so much because they've learned to use a squeegee. Do yourself the same favor. It's not that difficult. Besides, squeegees are cheaper in the long run.

Quick, relatively painless window washing depends on a squeegee. Squeegees are not in widespread use in homes, and that is a shame because of all the time they could save. One of the reasons for their disuse may be the awful quality of many of the squeegees in circulation. Those thick clumsy squeegees that are usually sold for use in cars are nearly worthless if you want a streak-free window.

You'll need a high-quality professional squeegee to get the job done right. We'll tell you how to select one and how to use it like a pro. Once you get the hang of it, you'll see how amazingly fast cleaning with a squeegee can be. Who knows? You may even begin to *enjoy* cleaning windows!

By now you must realize we're being pretty insistent about learning to use a squeegee. It's easier and faster, so why not? Trying to dry a windowpane by rubbing every square inch of it with messy newspapers or nonabsorbent, linty rags is hard work. *That's* what makes your arms hurt. *That's* what causes you to expend so much energy that you start to sweat. *That's* what causes accidents trying to stretch to reach the last few inches of a window (rather than using a simple squeegee on a pole). And *that's* a slow way to do something you don't even like doing.

MATERIALS

1 squeegee with 1 or more channels
1 double bucket (or a standard one)
1 squeegee scrub sleeve

10 cotton cleaning cloths
   clear ammonia or Cascade
1 wide paintbrush
1 variable extension pole up to 30 feet if necessary
1 pair of rubber gloves (optional)

Stock your Speed Clean apron with:

1 razor-blade holder with sharp blade
1 toothbrush
2 plastic bags as liners with clips

Two of these items deserve a bit of an explanation.

blade
channel
quick-release button
pivoting handle

Squeegee. The choice of the size of the squeegee is important. Obviously you don't want one wider than your windows. But you don't want a tiny one either, because you'd be making too many swipes. The size of the squeegee depends on the size of your windows.

We said earlier that you need a professional squeegee. One of the advantages of the professional model is that once you purchase the squeegee handle, several channels of different lengths are an inexpensive option. (A channel is the metal strip that holds the rubber blade.) You don't have to buy several different squeegees. You just slide one channel off and slide a different one on as needed. The one we use (an Ettore, manufactured by Steccone Products Co.) has a quick-release button that allows one channel to be switched with another in a matter of seconds. And the squeegee handle pivots to allow you to reach and clean windows at angles never before possible. This lets you wash windows easily despite having furniture or shrubs in the way.

If you have nothing but picture windows, get the widest squeegee you can handle comfortably: We recommend 18 inches. With little panes (like the ones in French doors) you obviously need a small one (about ⅔ the width of the pane). If you have medium-size windows, you're better off with a 14-inch channel. If you have a mixture of window sizes, the ideal solution may be two or more channels of different lengths.

The squeegee blade inside the channel is a thin strip of rubber with a very exacting edge—something like a heavy windshield wiper. However, just like windshield wipers, they can wear out because the edge becomes rounded with use and loses its effectiveness. The edge can also get nicked by hitting something when cleaning or if it's abused between uses.

A little nick that you might not even notice leaves a streak of water with every stroke of the blade. Luckily the replacement rubber blades are very cheap, so have a couple of extras on hand that fit the various channels you use (or just get several the size of your longest channel and trim them as needed). One nick leaving a streak with every stroke of the squeegee is downright discouraging. This is one reason why all those grocery-store squeegees are so unsatisfactory: The blades are soon nicked and damaged, but since they are not replaceable you have to throw the whole squeegee away and buy a new one just to get a new edge. This is also why these cheaper models really aren't.

Squeegee scrub sleeve. This looks sort of like a paint-roller cover with a slit in it so it can slide over the squeegee channel. It's used to apply cleaning solution to the window and scrub it at the same time. It pops off quickly (into the bucket) when you need the squeegee blade. The next best solution is a sponge or a cleaning cloth. However, neither work anywhere near as fast as a scrub sleeve. And if you have to use an extension pole they don't work at all without tying them to the squeegee.

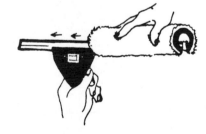

Getting Dressed

Tie the cleaning apron snugly around your waist. The apron is designed to keep you from driving yourself crazy running back and forth for items. It will hold the spare and retired cleaning cloths, razor blade, and debris you encounter. It will also hold a small squeegee. Put the paintbrush in your back pocket.

Preparing the Windowsills

If the interior windowsills are dusty, vacuum them first to avoid making mud. If the exterior sills are dusty, hose them down first to avoid muddy streaks running down the side of your home. You can't hose these streaks off after washing the windows for fear of splashing water and ruining your window-washing job. It's usually a good idea to dust or hose down both the interior and exterior sills. The alternative, if the dust is only slight, is to use the paintbrush that you are carrying in your back pocket. You can brush them off just prior to washing them. Include the frame, sill, and glass surface itself, if necessary.

The Cleaning Solution

We're going to give you a choice here between two very effective window cleaners.

- Cascade. This dishwashing detergent is a dandy window cleaner. It's very close to the formula that many professionals use. Its advantages are that: (a) it has chemical ingredients that help it rinse off the glass surface without streaking or leaving spots (remember all those TV commercials?); and (b) it evaporates from the window's surface a bit slower than an ammonia solution, so you have more time to work. Start with 1 tablespoon (liquid or powder) per bucket of water, or ½ tablespoon for one side of a double bucket.

• Clear nondetergent ammonia. Read the label carefully. Buy only clear, nondetergent, nonsudsing ammonia because suds are a real nuisance when washing windows—so much so that some professional window washers use just plain water. So use just a little: 2 tablespoons per full bucket or 1 tablespoon per half bucket.

Both Cascade and ammonia are alkali cleaners, and they will work excellently with about 95% of windows. But if the peculiarities of the dirt on your window do not respond well to either one of these, chances are that the dirt itself is alkali. You can outwit it by shifting to an acidic cleaner—plain white vinegar—about ¼ cup per full bucket. Don't use apple-cider or red-wine vinegar or you'll smell like a salad the rest of the day.

Fill a bucket (or one side of a double bucket) about half full with cool water. The water should *not* be hot because hot water evaporates too quickly on the window surface. On a cold day, when your hands are apt to turn blue, of course you would want the water to be on the warmish end of the scale. Wearing rubber gloves helps a lot when the weather is cold.

How much cleaning solution? Just enough to squeak by (sorry). Start with the amounts just mentioned. If your windows are appalling, replace the cleaning solution more often rather than increasing the concentration of cleaner. Only if you find the solution isn't working should you add more Cascade or ammonia.

BIG DECISION ONE:
Which side do I do first?

Wash the easiest side of the window first—that is, the side that has the easier access. By cleaning the difficult side last, if you see a smudge you'll know that it must be on the accessible side of the glass. If one side is in your nice warm dining room and the other side is exposed to winds howling across the East River, you would be well advised to start in your nice warm dining room., The idea is to have to venture out there only once.

In general, it's easier to wash all the windows from the inside if you can. There is usually shrubbery or some other obstacle in the way of the outside surfaces. Unless it's easy for you to clean there, stay inside when you can. (Read about your type of window, following.)

Choosing a Starting Point

Warm sunshine makes washing windows difficult because the heat of the sun evaporates the cleaning solution faster than you can squeegee it back off. The remaining solution turns into streaks, new dirt formations, or an unsightly film. When planning your strategy, arrange to start where the windows are shaded. An even better idea is to do the project on a cloudy day.

Final Details

Approach the windows armed with your equipment and a serene disposition.

Drape a cleaning cloth over one shoulder. Have the razor handy in the apron pocket and the brush in your pants pocket. Two or three spare cleaning cloths should be kept in another apron pocket. The scrub sleeve can be kept floating in the bucket between uses.

Put the bucket down to the left of the first window, if you can. Since there are all sorts of obstacles near and in front of windows, we don't care whether you start on the left or right as long as you have a reason for it. Putting the bucket all the way to the right or the left locates it in a place where you are not likely to step into it. Lean the extension pole, if any, against the frame of the window you're starting with—again, ideally in a place where you will not bump into it and make a spectacle of yourself.

In between uses, the best place for medium or large squeegees is inside the dry side of a double bucket. If you're using a conventional bucket, store it upside down on top of the bucket. Don't fill the bucket too full of cleaning solution or the squeegee handle will get wet. You don't want to splash water or start a clammy dribble down your arm. The handle will stay dry if it is suspended in this manner:

The first time you clean your windows using this method, move anything out of the way that's even close to being a disaster-waiting-to-happen. Move the lamp back a few more feet. Move the table in front of the window *completely* out of the way. Put the curtains on top of the curtain rods, etc.

As you develop some expertise using a squeegee, scrub sleeve, and extension pole, you'll find you can safely clean windows without moving much furniture at all. Then you'll save even more time and hassle. But accidents will happen until you're used to these tools, so move everything well out of the way this first time.

Getting Started

Let's wash the first window. Grab the wet scrub sleeve from the bucket. As long as you can reach all of the window, use the scrub sleeve by itself—i.e., not slipped onto the squeegee channel. That saves you time slipping it on and off the squeegee. In other words, you'll be using it like a brush. If the top of the window is out of reach, it's time to slide the scrub sleeve on the squeegee and use a long or short extension pole as needed.

If you're inside the house, shake or wring out the scrub sleeve so it doesn't drip cleaning solution all over. If you're outside, a little splashed water doesn't matter. The idea is to transport just enough cleaning solution to the window to cover it completely. The window should be just wet enough so it does not dry before you finish with the squeegee. If it's too wet, you'll make work for yourself later when water runs off the window onto the sill. To help manage dribbles of water, place a folded cloth on the windowsill below where the last stroke of the squeegee will end. It will catch any run-off and make drying the sill a snap.

Apply the cleaning solution with the scrub sleeve from top to bottom. Scrub a bit with the sleeve—just enough to loosen the dirt on the surface. But not too much scrubbing. Window dirt comes off very easily. Often, all you need to do is move the scrub sleeve lightly over the window once. You're doing little more than getting it wet, yet the window is now ready to be squeegeed clean and dry.

Then return the sleeve to the bucket and *don't dally*. Time is of the essence, because you have to start squeegeeing before the water evaporates from the window.

> ## THE MAJOR SECRET OF USING A SQUEEGEE
>
> **A squeegee blade must be dry and must be started on a dry surface each and every stroke.**

For the squeegee to work properly, it has to get a firm grip on the surface of the glass. That means a dry blade has to be started on a dry surface for each stroke. To accomplish this, dry a starter strip by hand at the edges of the window. Grab the cleaning cloth from your shoulder and use it to dry a 2-inch strip across the top and both sides of the window. Professionals call this step "cutting the water." The top strip is where you'll start the squeegee each stroke. The dry strips on the sides will help prevent water from oozing out from the window frames after the squeegee has passed by.

Now that you've dried the starter strips, make sure the squeegee blade is dry too. Wipe the edge of the blade with your cleaning cloth.

Place the squeegee blade down in the dry strip at the top of the window. Using a steady, *light* pressure, draw the squeegee down for the first stroke. "Light pressure" means not to have a death grip on the handle. A light and even pressure is what's needed because that's what works. It also keeps you from getting fatigued from what should be a simple task. Hold the handle with your fingers and thumb rather than in the palm of your hand. Don't grab it like a hammer. It will give you a lot more flexibility.

Stop the squeegee stroke a few inches from the lower window frame or bottom of the window. This avoids splashing water back onto the dry section if the squeegee were to hit the small puddle of water on the window frame. Your last squeegee stroke will get this strip. (See the illustration on p. 38.)

Wipe the squeegee blade dry.

Place it at the top of the window again, overlapping the first stroke by about 25%. Make a second pass with the squeegee down the window, again stopping a few inches from the lower window frame or bottom of the window.

Wipe the squeegee blade dry again and repeat the above steps until you have moved all the way across the window.

You have left a wet strip along the bottom of the window. Get it now, squeegeeing from side to side. That pulls the last of the cleaning solution into the corner. This is the corner where your cloth has been sitting waiting to catch this dirty solution. Smart, huh?

An equally fast way to wash the window is to make your squeegee strokes go across the window instead of up and down—provided that the window is not so large that you have to take steps while squeegeeing from one side to the other. You can go from right to left or left to right, depending on what's in the way. Cut the water on the top and on whichever side you'll be starting the squeegee. Start at the top and work your way down row by row. Remember to place a cloth in the corner of the sill toward which you'll be squeegeeing most of the water. If you produce prodigious puddles, wring out the scrub sleeve a bit more before doing the next window.

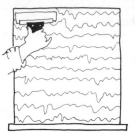

Wash the easy side first. Start at the top and hit all the corners well.

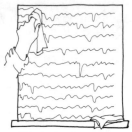

Wipe a 2-inch starting strip along the top and sides with a cloth. Place a folded cloth in the corner where most of the water will end up.

Wipe the blade dry. Make the first stroke. Stop a few inches from the bottom.

Wipe the blade dry. Make the second stroke, overlapping by 3 to 4 inches.

Wipe the blade dry. Make the third stroke.

Wipe the blade dry. Draw the squeegee sideways for the final stroke.

Small Matters

Occasionally, evaporation creates dry areas by the time you're ready to squeegee. So once you've covered the entire pane, you might have to give portions of the window a quick swipe with the scrub sleeve to rewet them. Plan on using more water outside than inside because of evaporation.

If the top of the window is out of reach, cut the water with the squeegee instead of a cloth. Lift the squeegee at an angle so that only about 2 inches of one end of the blade rests on the glass. Unless you're very fussy, for *outside* windows don't bother to cut the water on the sides of the window at all—just the top. The top is by far the most important area, since water dripping from there will travel all the way down the middle of the window. But if you skip the sides, the water that you miss will be scarcely noticeable.

Remember, the squeegee must be dry and must be started on a dry surface. Abuse of this simple rule is the main reason that people have difficulty with squeegees. The squeegee will not work properly if you start it on a wet surface or if its blade is wet when you start a stroke. In either case, the blade will sort of water-ski across the surface (hydroplane, to be more precise) instead of pushing the cleaning solution and dirt ahead of it, and streaks will appear without fail.

Also, *you've got to wipe the blade at the end of each stroke,* so don't fight it. It's sometimes awkward to dry the whole blade in one stroke because the cloth may catch on the ends of the blade. If you are having this trouble, first dry from the middle of the blade to one end. Then go back to the middle and dry to the other end. Two quick swipes.

Pull the squeegee in a smooth, continuous stroke. Don't start and stop. If you lift the squeegee off the surface, you've got to redry it and start again in a dry spot *ahead* of where you stopped. You won't make a streak provided the blade is dry. Soon it will become a reflex to make a complete stroke from top to bottom without stopping or lifting the squeegee.

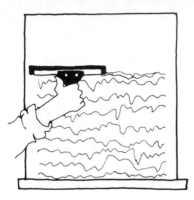

Very Large Windows

If the window is so large or the weather is so hot that the water evaporates too quickly to clean in a nonfrantic manner, just do half at a time. Start with the top half, of course. Squeegee as just described, but stop midway. Then wet the bottom half, and remember to start the squeegee in a dry spot. As long as you do this it won't streak, and you'll have as clean a window as if you did it all in one step.

Window Frames

We like to clean the window frames as long as we're going to all this trouble. The bottom edges of a window frame get pretty grimy, and this is a great time to tackle them as we're getting them wet anyway. Do only the lower frames, not all four sides, unless they really need it. (This is in addition to the rinsing or vacuuming that you did earlier.)

Do the frames just before you wash the window glass. First, wet the lower frame by passing one end of the scrub sleeve over it. Now quickly run your toothbrush over the frame, paying particular attention to the corners. Pop your toothbrush back into your apron pocket and wipe the frame clean and dry with a cleaning cloth. If you have trouble getting the dirt out of the corners after you've loosened it with your toothbrush, wash it out by squirting it full blast with Red Juice and then use a cloth to blot up the excess. Now wash the window. If a little cleaning solution gets on the frame as you wash the window, blot it up when you finish and move on.

Double-Hung Windows

If you have this type of window, nobody has to tell you that the outside can be a pain to clean. Here are four ways to clean the outside surfaces—most definitely in order of preference.

Method 1. Luckily, many double-hung windows are installed next to each other. This allows you to sit in one windowsill and wash and then squeegee the outside of the window next to it.

To follow this method, raise one lower pane as high as it will go to allow you to sit on the windowsill (careful!). You may need a short extension pole for this chore. A variable 2- to 4-foot extender or a sawed-off broom handle will both work. Set the bucket close to you but off to one side so you'll have a fairly good chance of not stepping into it later. Sit in the windowsill and reach to the neighboring upper pane to clean it first. The pivoting Ettore squeegee handle is perfect for this chore as it allows you to reach and clean at angles not possible with a fixed-position handle.

This is a time when it's a real joy to have an assistant to hand you things. If you don't have someone to press into service, be sure to locate all your equipment so you can reach it *before* you've gone through all the gyrations necessary to get settled in that windowsill.

Cut the water using the edge of the squeegee if you can't reach the top of the window with a cloth.

Clean and squeegee the top and bottom of the window next to you. Climb off the windowsill (careful!) and lower the window. Now trade places and sit in the windowsill of the window you just cleaned. Clean both the upper and lower panes of the second window from your new perch.

Precautions

If you're sitting on the sill holding on to the window frame for support, be sure the frame is strong enough to support you. It's not unusual for an old frame to have a nice coat of paint over it that effectively disguises visible signals that it's decayed and weak. If you're 15 feet or more above the ground, you should use a safety rope. Even with a safety rope, don't think you're invincible and lean out any farther or take chances you wouldn't ordinarily take. It's also a good idea to tie a string to the squeegee in a similar fashion so it won't fall on someone if you inadvertently drop it.

Even if it can't hit anyone as it falls, the string will save the squeegee from ruin and will save you from having to retrieve it.

Please remember to use proper safety precautions. We cannot recommend that you hang out on a ledge twenty stories above a sidewalk just to clean your windows. If it's unsafe to do so, stay inside and do the best you can.

Method 2. If you're unable to use Method 1 because there is only one window or because the window has a difficult shape (e.g., a bay window), you will have to wash it from the outside. We much prefer to clean from the outside—as in Method 1—as it is easier, it is more comfortable, and there are fewer obstacles. But sometimes you don't have a choice.

Method 3. If you can do neither of the above, you're down to your last two choices. For this method to work, both windows *must* move up and down for their full range of motion. If they cannot, skip ahead to Method 4—your last hope.

Many double-hung windows won't cooperate, especially if they've been painted a number of times or if the wood has swollen with moisture. This is particularly true of upper windows, which often only move an inch or two. *Don't force a stuck window!* The glass can shatter right in front of you. If windows must be repaired, call on a carpenter for help.

If both windows will open fully, here's how this method works. (Remember, this is all about the *outside* of the windows.)

Step A. First pull the upper window all the way down. Next raise the lower window high enough so there is just enough room for your arm to reach out between it and the top of the window frame. Wash and squeegee the top half of the lower window.

Step B. Push the upper window back into its normal closed position and raise the lower window all the way. Sit on the windowsill and clean the upper widow. Come back inside. It's a wonderful idea to have an assistant around to hand you items such as the scrub sleeve or squeegee as you need them. It's quite discouraging to get

Method 3

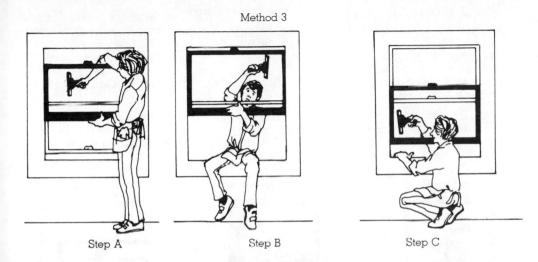

Step A   Step B   Step C

settled—only to realize you need something from inside and have to climb in and out all over again. Once you're settled, it's far more gratifying just to yell at your assistant.

Step C. Last, pull the lower window back down until you have just enough room to reach out between it and the windowsill and wash the bottom half of the lower window. You're done.

Do your best with this awkward but workable situation. Please observe the same precautions as in Method 1. In addition, when you are reaching out at Step A, make sure your center of gravity stays *below your waist.* Or your assistant can hold you. For added stability, Step C is usually best performed while on your knees.

Method 4. Many—perhaps a majority—of older double-hung windows have lost their full range of movement. If you can't pull the upper window down far enough to carry out Method 3, there is one last chance (short of taking off the sash and trim and removing the window to clean it). However, this method requires nearly as much window movement as Method 3.

If they don't open, they don't open. It's not the end of the world. Call a window-washing company and go fishing.

Step A. Unlike Method 3, all the steps in this method are done while you are sitting on the sill. So raise the lower window all the way and sit on the windowsill. Pull the upper window down as far as it will go. This allows you to reach up and wash the top

Method 4

Step A   Step B   Step C

half of the lower window. As with Method 3, this is ideally done with the help of an assistant who will hand you items you need.

Step B. Without moving from the sill, push the upper window all the way back up to its normal closed position and wash and squeegee it.

Step C. Finally, pull the lower window down until it just about touches your legs. This exposes the lower half of the window so you can wash it now. Then all you must do is extricate yourself from your perch and go back inside.

Again, we must ask you to observe the safety precautions discussed above, plus any others that occur to you as a reasonable person.

Sliding Aluminum Windows

If your house has sliding aluminum windows, normally one side will lift out. It's the movable half of the window that lifts up and out. Some do so only if they are in a certain position—usually just an inch or two open.

The sequence to follow when washing them is first to remove the half that comes out. Set it on the floor to one side or the other of the stationary window. Turn it around as you set it down, so the outside is facing you. Be careful when leaning it against the wall since the top edge will mark the wall. Protect the carpet also, because the bottom of the frame is often filthy. Use a couple of old towels to protect the floors and the walls.

Wash the outside of the stationary half of the window. You will normally need a short extension pole. Use it only for the part of the window you can't reach by hand (see the next section).

Next wash the outside of the window you removed. Clean it where you've leaned it against the wall, so you don't transport the window all over the house looking for a better place to clean it. Make sure it's stable, and use as little cleaning solution as possible to wash it. Then put the window back in and clean the inside of both windows if you haven't done so already.

The Extension Pole

An extension pole can make window washing a lot simpler and faster because you don't have to reposition a ladder constantly. But you do lose that direct hands-on control of the squeegee that you have when using it by hand. Accordingly, use the extender only for the part of the window that's outside your reach. First wash all of just that part of the window. Then put the extender away and wash the rest of the window without it.

When using the pole, be even more cautious about what's behind you. Step back from the window to give yourself a comfortable position. Cut the water at the top of the window by using one end of the squeegee blade at an angle. If you're using a long pole or if you're working in a tight space, this may prove difficult. The squeegee handle we use has an adjustable angle, which makes this job much more bearable.

Keep a mild, steady pressure on the pole. Sometimes it can begin to vibrate if the window is very high off the ground. If so, slow down the rate at which you are making a pass with the squeegee and move your hands farther apart on the pole to give it more stability. As usual, wipe the blade dry at the end of every stroke. Don't dally or the window surface will begin to dry.

Paint

The best way to remove dried paint splatters is with a clean, unpitted razor blade when the window is wet. There are several justifications for this rule: Ammoniated water will help loosen the paint; razors generally don't scratch a wet glass surface; and dry paint scrapings are often difficult to remove from a dry window. A dirty razor blade (for example, one coated with grease from the last time you used it) will leave a smudge behind, so use a clean one.

To avoid scratches, keep the blade at as low an angle as possible and use very slight pressure. Needless to say, do not use a razor blade on a plastic window.

Gummy Residue

Just about the only thing that is likely to give a razor blade a hard time on window glass is something gummy like the leftovers of tape or a label. If the razor on a wet surface doesn't work, squirt some lighter fluid on the offending glob and then try the razor. You'll probably be amazed. Wipe off any solid residue with a swipe of a cloth.

Squeegee Troubleshooting

If streaks remain after squeegeeing, there may be oil or grease on the glass. Try shifting to Red Juice, which specializes in cutting through oils. Then follow with a quick rinse with Blue Juice to remove any residue.

If Red Juice fails to banish the streaks, too, you may have to resort to a little friendly chemistry. Surprisingly often, streaks come from paint around the window frames—just like gilt can transfer from gilded frames to mirrors. The cleaning solution removes a tiny amount of the paint from the window frame and spreads it out over the window surface, much to your continued annoyance. This is far less likely to happen when using a squeegee, which is reason enough to use one.

Some paints (especially exterior latexes) are *designed* to generate a chalky layer on their surface that washes away and keeps the surface clean. Trouble is, of course, that it's that much easier to spread to the windows. If your window frames have this type of paint or any older paint in general, the problem can be exacerbated by using an alkali cleaner (Cascade, ammonia) because alkalis are particularly good at breaking down paint.

What to do? First, you'll have to be meticulous when wiping or squeegeeing around problem paint. If you wipe an edge, don't wipe the middle of the window with the same cloth without turning the cloth to a new section. You might also try shifting to white vinegar (an acid) for the cleaning solution, which may provoke the paint less.

Another cause of persistent streaks after using a squeegee is a worn-out blade. Inspect the edge of the rubber blade carefully. Often you will find a small nick in the

blade that will allow cleaning solution to be left behind as the squeegee is drawn down the window. If so, reverse or replace the blade. Also, keep a supply of spare blades handy. They're inexpensive, and you need a good blade if you're going to do this right. The rubber in the blade can become brittle with age, which is another reason to replace it. To prolong its useful life span, store the squeegee away from oils of any kind and out of direct sunlight.

To change the rubber blade, first notice that the rubber is held in place with a little brass clip at each end. Grasp one end of the old blade with a pair of pliers and pull or stretch it until the clip is exposed. Remove the clip and set it aside. Pull out the blade from the opposite end, saving the clip from that end also. Pay attention to how the clips were positioned so you'll be able to replace them in the same way for the new blade. Next take a new blade and slide it into the channel. If you must trim the replacement blade, cut it about ¼ inch longer than the channel. Place one clip on one end of the new blade. Push both the clip and the blade back into the channel, which locks one end in place. To install the clip on the other end, first stretch the blade by pulling on it with pliers. Put the second clip in place and release the blade. If necessary, push on the clips until they are seated properly. If the new rubber blade isn't perfectly flat, remove the clip from one end and reposition it a little farther from the end of the blade before reinstalling it.

Another place where streaks often form is along the sides of the windowpane. This can happen if the squeegee puts insufficient pressure on the very ends of the blade or if the ends are rounded or torn. Again, replace it as needed. Another cause of streaks along the sides is one tip riding up on the window frame as you draw the squeegee blade down the window. Keep your eye on the *end* of the blade nearest the frame as you draw it down the window. Don't watch the frame or the squeegee handle. That way the blade won't wander as easily onto the frame. If you do leave a little water at the edge of the window, don't try to touch it up. Just let it dry and you'll never notice it. People look out the middle of the window, and no one is going to inspect or notice the very edge of the window itself. If they do, hand them a squeegee.

Probably the most serious window problem, besides a Frisbee through the middle, is a persistent etching or fogging of the glass that resists any liquid cleaner or even the razor blade. It's not your imagination. Hard water marks, auto exhaust, run-off from unsealed masonry, pollution, or acid rain could be at fault. You may have some luck with a professional acid wash intended specifically for such problems.

Touching Up

Generally speaking, don't. A drip of water in the middle of your clean window will dry to an almost invisible dot. But trying to wipe it off with a damp cleaning cloth whose loose ends are slapping against the window in several places can quickly turn that little unnoticed dot into a window that you need to start all over with.

If you have streaks or spots that you must correct, use a little cleaning solution applied with your finger directly on the offending area and then a completely dry cleaning cloth to wipe it off again.

Squeegee Psychology

Cleaning windows with a squeegee can be an exasperating or a relaxing experience, depending on the pressure you are placing on the blade . . . and your nerves.

Inanimate objects typically do not respond well to force. The squeegee actually needs only the slightest pressure—just enough to keep it on the surface evenly. If you're pushing too hard, it will let you know and squeal as you move it down the window. It may also streak because too much pressure can cause the blade to distort and partially lift off the surface. Moreover, your hand will wear out in no time. So make a conscious effort to relax, and you may even enjoy yourself before long!

Super-Squeegeeing

Okay, you've got the basic squeegee technique down, but something's still missing in your window-washing life. You've noticed that hotshot professional window washers can squeegee windows in one long continous stroke back and forth across the window. They don't ever stop or lift the squeegee. You are jealous. Or you just want to torment the neighbors by showing off. Whatever your reason (or lack thereof), once you've mastered the basic technique and would like to make some fancy moves with the squeegee, forge on.

The basic idea of the advanced technique is simple. It's just that working out the kinks will require a bit of practice. And a loose wrist. Sorry to report it, but it's all in the you-know-what.

This technique is really practical only if you're cleaning larger windows. If they're smaller, the extra gyrations aren't worth the effort.

The plan is to complete the whole window with one continuous stroke of the squeegee, never picking it up off the surface of the window. First cut the water a few inches on top and at both sides. Professionals use only their squeegee for this task—not a cleaning cloth.

Next, place the squeegee vertically along the side starter strip in the upper corner of the window. Move it sideways until you get near the other corner, and then angle the upper end of the squeegee into it. Now rotate the blade—without lifting it off the surface—and head back in the other direction, overlapping the first stroke by a few inches. As you reach the other side, pivot the blade again and head back across. You're making giant sideways figure eights without ever lifting the squeegee from the surface. Angle the squeegee again into the first bottom corner you encounter and then do the last sideways stroke.

Of course it's going to be awkward the first few times. If you mess up, just dry the blade and start up again on a dry part of the glass. The corners and pivoting are going to be the hardest spots. Just keep loose as a goose: Remember, no death grip on the handle—no white knuckles. Hold the handle more toward the ends of your fingers rather than the palm of your hand, which will encourage flexibility in your grip. And don't be afraid to move that elbow. If you can remember, keep a slightly greater pressure on the upper part of the blade as you move to the left or right, which will help eliminate streaks and skipped spots.

When you've mastered the technique, plan your ambush of the neighbors carefully. It will be worth all the practice to be able to show off your new expertise.

BIG DECISION NUMBER TWO:
Are there any times when I should
use Blue Juice and cleaning cloths
instead of a squeegee?

For the vast majority of windows, the squeegee is the way to go. But there are a few situations in which it is necessary to clean with Blue Juice and a cloth.

Blue Juice and a cleaning cloth are sometimes faster than a squeegee if one of the following conditions prevails:

1. the window has an uneven surface (e.g., leaded glass or fake leaded glass windows);

2. the window only needs a touch-up (a fingerprint or two); or

3. you have only a few very small windows.

If a squeegee is ruled out and you must use Blue Juice or any other spray-on cleaner, remember these simple rules: Spray as little as possible in an even pattern over the window; work your way from top to bottom with big side-to-side strokes, turning the cloth as needed; use your razor blade on impossible spots like dried paint; and to avoid streaks, keep wiping until *all* the liquid disappears from the surface. A streak is leftover dirt and/or cleaning solution. So use only the driest and cleanest cloths you have. And use the cloths generously. When a cloth gets noticeably damp, toss it and grab a new one. Using dry cloths makes the job go much faster. The cloths will all fit into one load in the washer anyway.

If the window is only slightly dirty or if you need only to spot-clean a smudge or two, save time by spraying the cloth itself (lightly) and wiping just the smudge.

Spray Cleaner Troubleshooting

One of the reasons we are so fond of squeegees is that a whole flock of problems can arise when using a liquid spray and a cloth. For starters, make sure you wipe carefully in corners and along the edges, because that's where most misses happen.

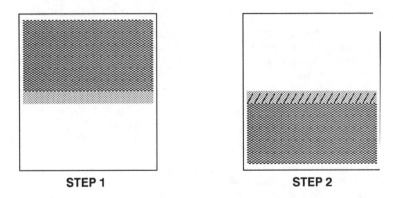

STEP 1   **STEP 2**

= Spray and wipe
= Spray but don't wipe
= Wipe only (you just sprayed it)

Sometimes the spray cleaner will evaporate before you get to a section to wipe it. If so, just spray and clean the top half of the window before doing the bottom. While you're at it, because you will be overlapping the top and bottom, you can save time by not wiping the lower 6 inches as you clean the top section. You will shortly be respraying it, so there's no need to clean it twice.

The same principle applies if you are cleaning adjoining windows. When you're cleaning the first window, overspray the next window about 6 inches so you can keep clear of the window you just finished when you move on to the next one. The idea is to avoid having spray drift back onto the window you just cleaned when you're spraying the next one. So:

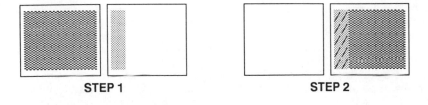

STEP 1　　　　　**STEP 2**

▓ = **Spray and wipe**
░ = **Spray but don't wipe**
╱ = **Wipe only (you just sprayed it)**

This looks a lot more confusing than it is in practice. All you're doing is saving yourself work by not recleaning areas you just finished.

5   WASHING CEILINGS

We believe that most ceilings should be washed about as often as you have your appendix out. Dirty feet do not walk on them. Dirty hands do not grab or poke them. Dust doesn't settle on them. Paintings are not hung on them, so there aren't rectangular clean spots and nail holes every few feet. Besides, unless your room has lighting that draws attention to the ceiling, people generally don't look up nearly as often as they look down or at eye level. So entire catastrophes can flourish on the ceiling and scarcely be noticed.

If dirt is distributed evenly over the entire ceiling, leave well enough alone. To be able to see dirt on a ceiling that is uniformly dirty, you would have to wash a spot so you could compare the dirty area to the clean area. Go ahead and clean or even paint the walls alone (if they need it). A nice, even coat of orange nicotine smoke damage will scarcely be noticed if left undisturbed. *You* may know better but your guests will not, and you can gaze upward with a sublimely ironic smile on your face.

If you clean the walls (Chapter 6) without doing the ceiling, be sure not to disturb the ceiling's uniform appearance by wiping any little spots clean, trying to repair any little holes or other damage, or by getting cleaning solution on it from the walls.

If you paint your ceilings off-white and your walls a different color, often you won't even need to repaint your ceilings when you repaint the walls. This saves lots of time because the ceilings are far more difficult and messy to paint, and you have to move the furniture much more extensively. I've painted my front room several times without touching the ceiling. The ceiling is dirty, I'm sure, but as it looks just fine I'm leaving it very much alone. By having the ceiling a different color than the walls, you've created a color scheme in which the ceilings are *supposed* to look different from the walls. Wonderful! Make the dirt earn its keep.

Sensible Reasons to Wash a Ceiling

Uneven filth is another story. For example, mold on bathroom ceilings is inconsiderate enough to flourish in conspicuous patches instead of even colonies. And cooking grease that builds up on kitchen ceilings often does so in a pattern that centers on the stove. In such cases you have to do something about the ceiling.

Your course of action depends on a few factors. If the existing paint on the ceiling is gloss or semigloss and in good condition, your cleaning job is going to be easier. If it's flat paint or the paint coating is damaged (peeling, blistering, water-stained, cracking, etc.), the balance tips quickly in favor of repainting the ceiling.

If the course of action is to wash the ceiling, read on!

The Choice of Cleaner

The choice of cleaner and list of materials to clean ceilings are essentially the same as those for cleaning walls. If you've already read these sections in the chapter on walls (Chapter 6), skip ahead.

We use clear ammonia for washing the ceiling. Clear ammonia is nonsudsy, nondetergent, and non–everything else. It is perfectly clear in appearance, not cloudy, and is generally sold only in janitorial supply stores. There are many other possibilities, but ammonia works as well or better than anything else we've tried. And it's downright cheap. Its major drawback—as in the case of all ammonia formulas—is its ferocious odor, but its superlative cleaning qualities are hard to pass up. With all types of ammonia, make sure the area you're working in is well ventilated.

Mix 1 or 2 cups of ammonia per gallon of water. If you use cool rather than warm water, fewer fumes will drift your way. Our second choice is Red Juice. Our third choice is TSP (trisodium phosphate), which we actually prefer to ammonia when we are washing the ceiling in preparation for repainting. The TSP leaves the surface microscopically etched, which gives the new paint a better "bite" on the surface. The few streaks it leaves won't matter since you're just going to paint right over them anyway.

MATERIALS

      1 cleaning apron
10 – 15 cleaning cloths
      1 spray bottle of Red Juice
      1 toothbrush
      1 white scrub pad
      1 quart of clear ammonia (or Red Juice or TSP)
      1 sponge mop
      1 stepladder (optional)
      2 plastic drop cloths or bed sheets
      1 pair of plastic gloves
         several 0000 steel wool pads

How to Wash Ceilings

Whether you are washing gloss or semigloss paint in the kitchen or bathroom, or flat latex paint in some other room, there are two ways to proceed. The fastest way is to use a sponge mop. We'll talk about that method first. The second way is to work from a ladder. We don't recommend using a ladder except when it's not possible to clean with the mop. When might that be? If the ceilings are too tall for you to be able either to reach them or to apply adequate scrubbing pressure to the mop, then skip ahead to "Ladder or Chair Strategy" (p. 62).

Getting Started

Tie your cleaning apron snugly around your waist. Hang the bottle of Red Juice on its appropriate loop and put the toothbrush in its pocket. Load five to ten cleaning cloths in a large apron pocket, and put the steel wool and the white pad into a plastic-lined pocket. Set the sponge mop and the cleaning tray with its extra cloths and supplies just outside the door of the room you're cleaning. Take the bucket and the clear ammonia to the nearest convenient sink.

Mix about ½ cup of clear ammonia in about half a bucket of warm water. (Adjust this formula according to how dirty the ceiling is.) We prefer using one side of a double bucket for reasons that will shortly become apparent. Carry the bucket to the corner of the room you're about to clean. It doesn't really matter, but for uniformity we start in the left-hand corner of the room farthest from the door we will eventually exit from. Set the bucket down and spread a plastic drop cloth to catch the drips. Wet the sponge mop in the ammonia solution and wring the mop nearly dry.

Washing an Area

Wet the mop enough to actually wash the ceiling well, but not so wet as to provoke much more than an occasional drip: more like a light shower than a rainstorm. Be especially careful to avoid splashing water on the walls. Even though you may be washing them soon enough, dribbles of water left on the wall for a period of time make streaks that are difficult to remove. When you see water running down the wall, wipe it off with a cloth.

Clean a small section of the ceiling (1–3 feet square) each time you dip the mop into the cleaning solution. Stand with your feet 2 to 3 feet apart, as though you were taking a long step forward. Clean with a back and forth motion with the mop. Work without actually taking any steps: Move the mop back and forth with your arms only, taking a step to the side only to advance to the next dirty area.

WRONG

RIGHT

Drying Each Area

When you've cleaned a total area of about 3 by 3 feet, it's time to rinse the mop well and squeeze all the water that you can out of it. Then drape a cleaning cloth over the sponge mop and wipe the same area you just washed. The cloth will dry that area somewhat, but it also will absorb any little round drips that would otherwise sit up there and dry into little round spots. Running the cloth over it this way also removes additional dirt (you'll see it in the cloths) and other potential streaks that would have become apparent after the ceiling dries. The idea is to dry with the cleaning cloth before the ceiling dries on its own. On some ceilings, the standard cleaning cloths won't stay in place over the mop head because of the rough texture of the surface or the type of paint. In such cases, use an old terry-cloth towel draped over the mop instead.

When you advance to a new area to clean, overlap the last area by half the width of the mop head. Also overlap when drying with the cloth. Be careful with these overlap areas—especially on latex paint. It is easy to end up with border marks that materialize later and draw a perfect map of each little 3 by 3 foot square for the whole world to see.

Optional Rinsing

If the ceiling is extremely dirty you may have to rinse it. Normally, washing with the mop and then wiping with a cleaning cloth or towel is sufficient. Use your own judgment, but if you decide to rinse, this is how to proceed.

If you're using a double bucket, fill the second side with clear water. If you're using standard buckets, use a second one for rinse water. After cleaning each area, rinse the sponge mop in the cleaning solution, wring it dry, and then repeat in the clean rinse-water side of the bucket. After wringing it as dry as you do when washing with it, use the mop to rinse the area you just cleaned. Dump the dirty water often, or you will just redistribute the dirt. As soon as the rinse water is dirty enough to be able to be seen on the ceiling, it's time to dump it out and refill it.

Don't rinse unless you're sure it's necessary or you're not satisfied with the results without it. This step is seldom needed unless the ceiling is truly unspeakable.

Edges: If You're Also Washing the Walls

It's a little tricky to clean the ceiling along the edge, where the ceiling meets the walls. If you start your mop directly against the edge when it's full of cleaning solution, it is likely to drip on the wall beneath and you'll waste time having to stop to wipe the drips off. To avoid this difficulty, start with the mop about a foot away from the edge and work in toward the edge. (Painters call this motion cutting in when they're using a paintbrush.) Stand close to the wall while you're working.

Once you've worked the sponge mop against the edge, pay close attention so the sponge will get that last bit of the ceiling. As long as you clean each edge leading into a corner, you will automatically clean the corner as well.

Edges: If You're *Not* Also Washing the Walls

The above method of cleaning into the corner and along the edges of the ceiling will also clean the top two inches of the wall. If you *don't* want to wash the walls at this time, clean the edges and corners by hand to avoid that 2-inch-clean streak at the very top of the wall. If you don't mind that, fine.

You'll need a stepladder or a chair to do the work by hand. Be careful climbing up and down the ladder with things in your hand. But you don't have to haul the bucket up the ladder, just one of your cleaning cloths. First wet it in the ammonia solution, wring it out, and take it up the ladder with you. Use it to clean the last little area of ceiling near the wall and then wipe the area dry with another cleaning cloth.

It's a bit risky to change from the mop to a cleaning cloth because they clean somewhat differently and may leave a noticeable difference when the surface dries. This won't be a problem if you clean all but the last few inches of the ceiling with the mop. Then the small strip you hand-clean with a cloth will scarcely be noticeable—if at all. Clean as much as possible with the mop and as little as possible by hand.

How to Move the Furniture Only Once

Let's say you're working your way out from the corner and are about to bump into a chair that's directly in your way. If you're not careful, you'll end up moving that chair four times before you're done—especially if you will be washing the walls after you finish the ceiling. You will move it: (1) out to wash the ceiling; (2) back when you come to it again; (3) back out to wash the walls; and (4) back again when you're finished with the walls.

Don't waste all that time. Move it once out and once back as follows: When you come to the chair in the first place, don't move it at all. Instead, first wash the ceiling over the spot to which you intend to move the chair—usually just three feet straight ahead. Wipe the area dry and move the chair. Then clean the ceiling over where it was, wipe the ceiling dry, and keep on going. *Don't* move the chair back yet. When you come back in the other direction, the chair will be in your way again. But since you've already cleaned above the chair, just skip ahead to the next dirty area on the other side of the chair. Leave the chair alone until you are finished with the walls—if you are cleaning them at all. If not, return the chair to its original spot.

Remember to throw a drop cloth over furniture or countertops when you are cleaning close to them. Those little drips of dirty water cause stains that can be tedious to clean up. Also keep a drop cloth on the floor in the area you're working to protect the floor finish. For the floor, heavier cloths are much easier to manage — especially a real painter's canvas. They won't cling to you like plastic wrap when you walk on them. The lighter and thinner plastic ones are more suitable for countertops and furniture.

Light Fixtures

If you're lucky, you can usually figure out a way to clean around the light fixtures, using the same technique you use when cleaning a corner. Don't clean close to them when your mop is still dripping, and move your body around the fixture to clean it from different angles. If you're not able to clean it from the floor using your mop, then resort to a chair or ladder. If so, use a cleaning cloth to clean and a second cloth to wipe the area dry. As you're wearing a cleaning apron, you'll have a cloth in your pocket and won't have to climb back down the ladder to get one.

How Good Is Your Ladder?

If you have a rickety old ladder that has been called many things, but "safe" isn't one of them, use it for firewood and buy a new one. Or rent one. But don't take a chance on a broken leg or worse. If you are going to buy a new 5- or 6-foot stepladder, we prefer wood to aluminum. We assume this ladder is going to be used inside the house most of the time, and wood ladders tend to cause less damage even though they're heavier than aluminum ones. It's difficult to use the ladder all day—moving it a dozen times or more—without dinging a wall or woodwork or furniture. A wood ladder is more forgiving than an aluminum ladder when these minor collisions occur because it has more rounded edges. You also tend to move more deliberately with it because it's heavier. And besides, a wood ladder is more stable than an aluminum one.

Ladder or Chair Strategy

In some situations you cannot avoid using a ladder when washing ceilings. If the ceiling is too tall, first try using the mop while standing on a chair. Or if the ceiling is so tall that your mop is straight up in the air before you can reach it, then use a chair so you can work from an angle and avoid being right under your work area—and in the path of every drip. Select a chair that is sturdy and stable and not covered with anything slippery. If you need to protect the chair, cover it with a towel to ensure firm footing. If a chair won't do, use a ladder.

You probably already know a lot of the rules about using a folding stepladder. Don't stand on the top two rungs of the ladder. Don't use a stepladder unless the spreaders are fully opened and snapped in place to lock them. Set the bucket only on the little folding shelf that was designed for that purpose. Don't move the ladder while the bucket is still on the shelf. When working near a door, make sure the door is either wide open or else closed and locked. Don't lean your body off center to reach for something, or gravity will take over in a most unpleasant way.

An important aspect of ladder strategy is to do as little work as possible with a ladder alone. It's just about the slowest and most inefficient technique possible. Rather, we recommend that you set up a simple work platform to clean the ceiling. It will save having to move the ladder so many times, and it will mean you can clean the stairwell ceiling without risking life and limb.

Work Platforms
and Scaffold Planks

Either of the work platforms we show you, or your own variations thereof, require a plank to stand on. Ordinary planks won't do. They aren't strong enough, wide enough, thick enough, or long enough to be safe. You'll need a specialized scaffold plank. These are 2 inches thick by 8 inches wide (nominal size) and up to 10 feet long (actual size). They also come longer than 10 feet, but the longer lengths require additional support in the middle—not something realistic for the present purposes. If you are also going to use the plank to paint, or perhaps could use it outside for window washing, you might consider buying one at a lumberyard. Planks can also be rented at paint stores or many equipment-rental stores.

Here are two configurations that can be used to make life easier while working on ceilings or high walls—for washing or painting or wallpapering. One is a work platform. The other is a more specialized stairwell platform.

Work Platform

Unless your ceilings are unusually high, here is a simple work platform that will eliminate all those trips up and down the ladder and moving it so often. You may use a sawhorse plus your ladder, or two sawhorses. You can also use a chair, or even two chairs, as long as you follow the same rules that apply to the sawhorses and ladder: *Be sure the scaffold plank extends 1 foot beyond the edge of whatever it rests on.* Needless to say, the resulting platform must be level.

Don't make the whole thing unsafe by using something inappropriate to try to correct the height at one end of the platform—like a pillow (too wobbly), a pile of books (not wide enough), or a trash can (not strong enough). You get the idea. It's best to use a combination of things (sawhorse, ladder, and chair) so you don't have to add anything else to correct the height, which is just one more thing to take apart and move every time you need to change the location of the platform. If you must, a couple of safe things to use for leveling the platform are: a plank (2 inches by 6 inches or larger) cut into appropriate lengths, or one or two books if they are large enough (something like an encyclopedia).

Doing the Work on a Platform

Even though you are using a work platform, you proceed in pretty much the same way we described in the first part of this chapter. Prepare the same way, start in the same place, and use the same cleaning solution. However, instead of using a sponge mop, use a large hand-held sponge. We prefer the synthetic kind because their rectangular shape and smooth sides apply even pressure over a larger area than does a natural sponge. If you have a little sponge by the kitchen sink, or a dirty old sponge that you've been using to clean the car, and it constantly sheds bits of sponge because it's rotting away, you must know by now that we aren't going to let you use it for this job. Spring for a brand-new sponge about 4 inches by 6 inches in size. But don't buy a cheap one with no spunk. Get a substantial one. You'll thank yourself more than once.

When working on a platform, place the bucket beside you. Which side you choose depends on what hand you use to clean. If you're right-handed, locate the bucket on your right so you don't have to twist and turn to reach the bucket when working. (Such movements aren't as simple as they might sound when you're on a narrow plank above the floor.) Then work your way to the left so you don't run into the bucket, which could have spectacular consequences. If you're left-handed, kindly reverse these directions.

Rinse the sponge, wring it dry enough so that it isn't dripping, and use it to clean an area of the ceiling about 3 feet by 3 feet. Put the sponge back in the bucket and take a cloth from your apron pocket and wipe the same area dry. Even a very dirty wall or ceiling doesn't need to be rinsed using this method. Just be sure you wipe each area with a cleaning cloth right after you wash it with the sponge—and before the area dries on its own.

Stairwell Work Platform

Here is an illustration of how to erect a work platform in a stairwell in case that area has you stumped. Nothing else is different as far as cleaning procedures go, but please exercise extreme care when using an apparatus such as this in a stairwell.

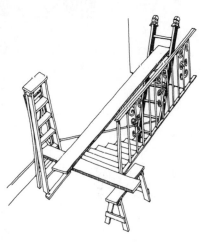

Porous Ceilings

If you have a fairly smooth, well-painted surface over a plaster or drywall ceiling (the most common types), you can usually clean it and be satisfied with the results without causing any noticeable damage to the surface.

Not so with many porous surfaces. Most of us are aware of how difficult acoustical ceilings are to wash—especially the blown-on variety. But stucco, some types of plaster, and textured concrete can also be damaged by your attempts to clean them. Or they may look no better. Don't try to wash these types of ceilings. Paint them instead or call in professional help. Or vacuum them if you're dealing just with loose soot or other particulate matter. You'll feel better. And then get back to whatever you were doing before the idea to wash them popped into your head.

If you have acoustical ceiling tiles, it is usually possible to wash them if you're careful and patient. There are specialty cleaning products for such ceilings, including dry sponges that rely on dry-cleaning chemicals and an absorbent surface material.

Those of you who have soft-blown acoustical ceilings know that they are just about impossible to maintain. The best you can hope to do is to use the soft long-bristle brush attachment with the vacuum to remove cobwebs and obvious dust or soot while trying not to dislodge more of the ceiling than is absolutely necessary. The only other possibility is to have it spray-painted. Hire a professional painter. Or move.

Maintenance

The proper way to maintain ceilings is largely preventive in nature. Unless the ceiling is unusually clean, you can't spot-clean it with your mop without a patch of cleanliness becoming very apparent.

Preventive maintenance involves finding and eliminating the source of recurring dirt. Chief offenders are undersized or clogged exhaust fans over kitchen stoves. Clean the fan filter religiously. It's not as hard as it looks: Pop it into the dishwasher. (See Chapter 14, "Getting the House Ready for Weekly Cleaning.")

Soot from exhaust vents are another annoyance. The first thing to do is check the filters in your heating/ventilating/air-conditioning (HVAC) system. If they're in good shape, it may benefit you to consult with an HVAC contractor to see what else can be done to reduce the soot level.

Mildew is a timeless enemy of ceilings. Moisture tends to condense on warm ceilings more than on other surfaces, and mildew needs moisture like we need air to breathe. Ventilation is your first line of defense. Use the fan if there is one. Make sure the bathroom window or door is kept open during a shower—or at least afterward, long enough to let heavy moisture dissipate. Mildew is a living organism, and once it takes hold on a surface it is tenacious. When you have to repaint the ceiling, use an oil- or alkyd-based primer plus top coat, each with a mildew-preventing agent added. It really does help. You might also consider an oscillating room fan to keep the air moving, which the mildew will not appreciate at all. Aim it toward the ceiling.

6 WASHING WALLS

It is an exceptional day indeed when you have to wash a wall completely. Certainly some walls would benefit from being washed, but it would be better to paint others instead, and some should be benignly ignored. Your decision about what to do will depend not only on the degree of uncleanliness, but also on the type of paint and type of surface as well.

Gloss and Semigloss Paints

These are the exceptions to our general disinclination to clean walls. Gloss and semigloss paints call for a thorough cleaning much more often than a repainting. They wash and clean up far more easily than flat paint, which is a primary consideration for selecting them in the first place. In this chapter we'll show you the fastest way to wash these walls.

Do a test area first to be sure that you will do no damage to the surface. The test also tells you whether or not the walls need cleaning to begin with. If they don't look any different after the test, relax and wait until next year.

Flat Paint

As you know, it's much more laborious to clean flat paint, and it's much less likely to come clean of fingerprints, stains, smoke, grease, and so forth. Nor does it do as good a job resisting damage by the chemical action of cleaning. The paint itself can be discolored or actually dissolved by the cleaning solution, or it can be worn right off the walls during the cleaning process.

Latex paints vary in several ways—ability to cover previous coats, resistance to fading, depth of color, resistance to running, and cleanability. Often to excel in one dimension the paint manufacturer must sacrifice one or more of the others. Cheaper flat latex paints are notorious for allowing stains to go right through the coating and for rubbing right off when you try to wash them. When you buy paint ask about its rated ability to be cleaned. It's often worth the extra dollar a gallon to get a premium grade of paint that will save you hours of work in the long run. You can also check the periodic reviews of house paints in consumer magazines.

But even if you bought an excellent grade of flat paint, its chief maintenance advantage is not that you can wash the entire surface of the walls. Rather, you are much more likely to be removing stains and spot-cleaning the small areas around the light switches and thermostat—hundreds of times during the lifetime of the paint, perhaps. But don't wash the entire wall! Only do this in case of emergency (like smoke damage) or your own personal choice—and to heck with our advice.

So what should be done with flat-finished walls that are thoroughly dirty? Paint them. Painting may not be cheaper, and it certainly involves hard work (as does washing them), but the walls will look so much better when you're finished. For a bit more effort, it's worth it and here's why.

Most of these flat-finished walls that you are thinking about washing have seen a fair amount of history enacted in front of them in their years of service. The wall behind the rocking chair has numerous little nicks where the chair has hit the wall over and over and over again. There's an infuriatingly visible scratch next to the picture frame that was gouged when you jiggled the frame as you were cleaning it. Then there are those holes in the wall where all the pictures used to be before you rearranged everything a couple of years ago—plus the holes left over from the Christmas decorations. Also the paint-free spots where you had taped up balloons for the birthday party last summer. Remember the sickening feeling when the tape took the paint right off the wall? Oh, and those oily patches where people lean their heads against the wall while they watch TV? And then there's the corner where the dog sleeps. And the red crayon stains that you can still see despite your best efforts.

Unfortunately, even after you've washed these walls, a great many of these eyesores will still be there. If you paint, they will be obliterated. With either job, you'll have to cover the furniture, move the furniture away from the walls, take down the pictures, and remove the drapes. This is a big chunk of work whether you're washing or painting. Paint. You'll be happier.

One exception to this rule is if you've had an accident in the room before all the normal wear-and-tear conflagrations have had a chance to transpire. Maybe some heavy-duty smokers turned the walls a shade of nicotine orange only a few months after you painted. Go ahead and wash the walls. Or maybe you moved into a house with walls so dirty that they have to be washed before you can even think of painting them. Or it may just be a matter of personal choice. If you feel better washing the walls, by all means go right ahead. The instructions follow.

The "inconspicuous test area" is even more important with flat latex surfaces. The chances of a bad reaction between the paint and the cleaner are greater than with other surfaces. Don't take a chance without trying the cleaner in an out-of-the-way spot first.

The Choice of Cleaner

We prefer clean, nonsudsy, nondetergent, non–anything–else ammonia for washing walls. There are many other possibilities, but ammonia works as well or better than anything else we've tried. And it's downright cheap. Get *clear* ammonia, which is generally sold in janitorial supply stores. Its major drawback—as in the case of all ammonia formulas—is its ferocious odor, but its superlative cleaning qualities are hard to pass up. With all types of ammonia, make sure the area you're cleaning is well ventilated.

Mix 1 to 2 cups of ammonia per gallon of water. If you use cool rather than warm water, fewer fumes will drift your way. Our second choice is Red Juice. Our third choice is TSP (trisodium phosphate), which we actually prefer when we are washing walls in preparation for repainting. The TSP seems to leave the surface microscopically etched, which gives the paint a better "bite" on the surface. The few streaks it leaves won't matter because you're just going to paint right over them anyway.

MATERIALS

        1 cleaning apron
  10 –15 cleaning cloths
        1 quart of clear ammonia (or TSP or Red Juice)
        1 sponge mop
        1 spray bottle of Red Juice
        1 toothbrush
        1 white scrub pad
          several 0000 steel wool pads
        1 stepladder or chair (optional)
        2 plastic drop cloths or bed sheets
        1 pair of rubber gloves

See If You Can Get Away
With Spot-Cleaning

Usually the only walls you ever need to wash are in the kitchen and bathroom. These rooms are normally covered with a gloss or semigloss paint that should respond well to cleaning. But often there are just a few streaks over a kitchen countertop, or a few lines on bathroom walls caused by condensation. Just wipe off these areas with Red Juice and a cleaning cloth when you're doing your normal weekly cleaning. Sometimes that's all that's really needed to keep them relatively spotless. The idea is to spot-clean absolutely whenever you can get away with it. If not, proceed with full washing. Most bathroom walls could use complete washing a couple of times a year, and the kitchen once a year or so.

Preparation

If this is a kitchen or bathroom, there usually isn't much furniture to move away from the walls. But regardless of the room, move the furniture that will be in the way and then pay particular attention to the small items. For example, move the garbage can out of the room so you don't collide with it later. Move or cover trays of little items like makeup and perfume so cleaning solution doesn't drip on them. Move items on the kitchen counters away from you or out of the way in case you have to stand on the countertops as you work.

Take down the curtains or drapes. And then, unless they are nice and clean, wash them or send them out to be dry-cleaned. The only time you don't have to take them down is when you aren't washing the window frames. But since the frames are usually just as dirty as the walls, that won't generally be the case. Okay, okay! You can leave the drapes up if it's too much of a hassle: if they are too heavy, or you won't be able to put them back up, or you just don't want to bother. But be aware that they will slow you down as you try to clean the woodwork under and around them if they are left in place. Get miniblinds out of the way by pulling them all the way to the top position—or send them out to be cleaned also. (Look in the Yellow Pages under "Venetian Blind Cleaners.")

Remove all the pictures from the wall. Don't remove the nails. Be careful, however; the nails practically disappear from sight once the pictures are off, and they turn into deadly little pieces of metal that slice fingertips and rip sponges. You can protect yourself from them by hanging a cleaning cloth from each nail as you remove the picture. The cloth will remind you where the nails are so you can avoid any mishap with them as you wash your way around the room. As you're using cleaning cloths anyway to dry the wall, you can put the cloths to work when you collect them back from the nails as you come to them.

If the windowsills and baseboards are even moderately dusty, vacuum them first with the brush attachment. It is extremely important that you take the time to follow this instruction. If your home is like many where the walls need washing, the baseboards and windowsills are also nice and dusty. You do remember what happens to dust when you add water to it. Mud. And it is much more tedious to remove mud by hand than it is to remove dust with a vacuum cleaner. Don't forget to vacuum the high molding. Cobwebs are much easier to vacuum away than to wash away—especially as they have a lousy little habit of swinging loose and landing smack in an area you just cleaned. Vacuum the walls themselves only if there is visible dust on a flat latex surface.

If You're Washing Walls *After* Washing the Ceiling

If you plan on doing the ceiling during the same session as the walls, do the ceiling first. (See Chapter 5, "Washing Ceilings.") If you've just finished washing the ceiling, go to the same corner in which you had started the ceiling. As the ceiling is now clean, you don't have to worry about disturbing the uniformity of its appearance. This means you can safely continue to use a mop on the walls all the way up to the ceiling.

Tie your cleaning apron snugly around your waist. Hang the bottle of Red Juice on its appropriate loop and put the toothbrush in its pocket. Load five to ten cleaning cloths in a large apron pocket, and put the steel wool and the white pad into a plastic-lined pocket. Set the sponge mop and the cleaning tray with its extra cloths and supplies just outside the door of the room you're cleaning. Take the bucket and the clear ammonia to the nearest convenient sink.

Mix about ½ cup of clear ammonia in about a half a bucket of warm water. (Adjust this formula according to how dirty the wall is.) We prefer using one side of a double bucket for reasons that will shortly become apparent. Carry the bucket to the corner of the room you're about to clean. It doesn't really matter, but for uniformity we start in the left-hand corner of the room farthest from the door we will eventually exit from.

Strategy

This is back to basics, but Rule 1 applies—Work around the room once without backtracking. Clean everything as you come to it—upper molding, door frames, windowsills, and lower molding—not to mention the walls also. Work to the right and from top to bottom as you proceed. Use the mop to wash, and a cleaning cloth over the mop to dry. As with ceilings, save time by not rinsing except in extreme cases.

Work from the Top Down!

Just about every book we've read on the subject, and every person we've ever talked to, says to wash walls from the bottom up. The stated reason is because streams of cleaning solution run down the wall and cause anxiety-provoking streaks. Right, but don't you have exactly as many dribbles of cleaning solution running down the wall if you work from the bottom up? Of course you do. The same number of dribbles are going to travel the same paths—in one case on a dirty surface, in the other on a clean surface. Streaks may appear to be catastrophic at first, but eventually they blend into the background as the cleaner takes effect on the whole surface. The only danger is when dribbles are left on the wall for a long period. In that case, you'll be making work for yourself by having to blend them into the background. The correct technique is to *manage* the cleaning solution on the wall. When you see solution running down the wall, wipe it off with a cloth before it has a chance to cause trouble.

Besides, if you work from top to bottom you don't have to retouch the bottom as much. For example, if you clean the baseboard first, and then clean the wall above it, there is no way in the world you can clean that wall without dripping dirty cleaning solution onto your nice clean baseboard. So you have to stop and wipe the baseboard you just cleaned. How much smarter and quicker to wash the wall first from top to bottom and then wash the baseboard last—never having to worry about little drips splattering on your clean work. As Rule 3 says: Work from top to bottom. Always. Period. Don't argue.

Use the Mop

Stand a couple of feet from the wall so you can reach into the area you are cleaning with the mop. That is, don't try to wash the area right in front of you. Wash a strip about 3 feet wide and proceed all the way from the top of the wall down to the baseboards before you move ahead to the next strip. Stop to rinse the mop as often as necessary. If the room is too small, or the wall is too hard to reach because of immovable objects, you can take the sponge head off the mop and use it by hand. Or use a cleaning cloth or sponge on small areas. Keep the amount of cleaning solution running down the wall to a minimum by wringing the mop thoroughly after you rinse it.

Wiping Dry

Each time you finish a strip of the wall with the mop, rinse the mop head out, wring it as dry as you can, and put a cleaning cloth over it. Now use it to wipe that same area dry. This is the same technique used when doing the ceiling. Just run the cloth over the wall, holding the mop the same way as you did when washing. Stop and turn the cleaning cloth or put on a new one as often as necessary. It's important to keep the cloths uniformly dry and uniformly clean so the wall will have an even cleanliness after it dries. Wipe with the cloth before the walls dry of their own accord or else you'll end up with streaks. If you have trouble keeping the cloths in place, use old terry-cloth towels instead.

Lower Part of the Wall

After you clean the upper part of the wall that's out of reach, you will find it easier to stop using the mop entirely. At lower levels, the mop handle can start to become awkward to maneuver, especially in small or crowded rooms. You can remove the sponge from the mop and use it alone, or you can use a large sponge or a cleaning cloth dipped in cleaning solution.

Baseboards, Molding, Doors, and Windows

You have to wash them. They won't go away. And it's fastest to clean them as you come to them. By cleaning them in turn, you don't waste time backtracking or making additional trips around the room to do them later.

Nooks and Crannies

Clean areas that are difficult to reach with your toothbrush. It works very well in the corners of windowsills or woodwork, around (and on) light switches, molding, and stubborn spots. No need to be dainty with it either. You can really agitate up a storm with it and cover a surprisingly large surface fast. Switch to a larger brush if you have to cover substantial square footage. Just keep it moving. If you need a little extra cleaning solution in an area, reach for your Red Juice rather than the bucket or mop.

Corners

These are easy. Just stand close to each wall in turn to clean all the way into the corner. First do one side all the way to the baseboards and then the other side all the way down. Then clean the corner baseboards and wipe the area dry.

If you can't get into the corner all the way because of the size of the room or some other obstacle, grab a cloth and use that instead.

Spots and Stains

The toothbrush and Red Juice are your first line of offense against spots and stains. If they fail, recall that you are carrying a white pad and fine steel wool. If you come upon a relatively innocent little black mark on the wall, say ¼ inch wide and 1 inch long, please *don't* grab your steel wool and start scratching away at an area of the wall that measures a good 6 by 6 inches. That method may indeed remove the small black spot—the one that none of your friends could see without their glasses—or it could turn it into one that you can't miss from the next room. Be careful.

When using a white pad or steel wool pad on a spot on the wall, the idea is to concentrate its effectiveness on the spot and not the surrounding area. This is accomplished by applying pressure with your finger on the pad on just the spot. You can even use something like the handle end of the toothbrush to concentrate the working surface of the pad.

We are frequently asked how to remove crayon marks from walls. Our method is to spray the area with Endust, agitate gently with the toothbrush, and wipe with a cleaning cloth. Then spray the same area with Red Juice to remove the Endust residue. Wipe clean and dry. The Endust works its way under the crayon mark and floats it off the surface. We have used this method on scrubbable painted walls as well as many types of wallpaper (especially vinyl). Again, you must pretest an area to make sure the procedure is safe for your particular wall surface.

Managing the Cleaning Solution

Change it often. If you don't, you will be able to see plainly the difference between a clean and dirty solution on the walls.

You're Finished!

If you persevere you will complete one trip around the room, which means that you're finished. Congratulations!

**If You're Washing Only the Walls
and *Not* the Ceiling**

When you clean or paint the walls without doing the ceiling, be sure not to disturb the uniform appearance of the ceiling or it will be painfully obvious. The reason a dirty ceiling may still look just fine is that the dirt on it is undisturbed. For example, if you molest that even layer of smoke on the ceiling by splashing water on it or by inadvertently cleaning a streak here and there with the mop, you'll make some brilliantly clean spots that are much worse than nice even dirt because now you'll have to wash the entire ceiling. There are better ways to spend Saturday afternoon.

The way to avoid touching the ceiling when cleaning the walls is first to clean the top foot or so of the wall with a cleaning cloth or a sponge, using a second cloth to wipe the area dry. Then use the much faster mop to wash the rest of the wall. Standing on a chair if you can—a ladder if you must—clean the strip at the top of the wall. But don't do the strip all the way around the room. Rather, clean a strip that you can reach from the chair and then move the chair ahead and wash the rest of the wall with the mop. (You're just working from the top to the bottom before moving on.) Except for this strip, follow the wall-washing instructions for mops that we have already described. Be very careful not to touch the ceiling at all.

Washing Walls Using a Ladder
or Work Platform

There are times that you must use a ladder to wash walls. Let's say you don't believe us about how well the sponge-mop method works, or the dirt is such that you can't scrub hard enough with the mop, or the walls are too high. There is no way to avoid a ladder. So be it.

The basic strategies are almost identical to those used while using a ladder or a platform to wash ceilings, which are discussed in Chapter 6, "Washing Ceilings." No sense repeating them here, but there are one or two considerations peculiar to walls that we should review.

Do the Top Half of the
Wall First

Because the work platform will be in the way of cleaning the bottom half, you can wash only the top half of the wall on the first pass. As before, be sure to catch or wipe off streaks of cleaning solution that start to run down the wall. Clean the top half of the wall from one end of the work platform to the other, and resist the temptation to reach or lean past the end or you may upset the whole apple cart. Then set the bucket on the floor near the first part of the wall you washed from the platform.

Move the platform by moving the plank first, and then each chair or ladder. Next wash the lower half of the wall, including the baseboards. Then get back up on the platform and start again on a new section. Clean window frames, sills, door frames, and any other woodwork as you come to them.

Once again, after you've made one complete trip around the room, you're done.

Maintenance

The proper way to maintain walls is to keep them free of spots and fingerprints. Each time you do your weekly cleaning, have Red Juice at the ready for new spots that have appeared. Remove them by spraying and wiping clean with a cloth. Anything that gets on the wall that might result in a permanent stain should be removed whenever you see it. Don't wait until you clean the house again.

The other maintenance is preventive in nature. Especially when you wash a wall, you'll discover things that could have been done to make the job easier. For instance, if the furnace vent is making a black area on the wall above it, install an air deflector. Oily spots on the wall from hair can be avoided by locating a pillow at strategic spots on the couch. If the chair is hitting the wall, move it out and put something under the legs so it doesn't move right back. As you clean house, be aware of spots being made on the walls that can be stopped by moving something. Then do it. It's a pleasant feeling to solve these little problems instead of just wondering about them as you're cleaning. You'll be grateful you did because the house will look better between now and when you wash or paint again—and those jobs will be that much easier too.

7 FLOOR COVERINGS

Before you can make a sensible decision about the type of treatment for your floors, you'll need to know what type of floor covering you are dealing with. In the sections that follow, we will first give a short primer on each of the major types of residential floor coverings. (Sorry, no Astroturf.) The descriptions are especially intended for those of you who have moved into a house and are not sure of the type of floor covering installed previously. Please bear with us if the terminology is not exactly the same as a flooring contractor or salesperson might use, as terms for products in this field are changing constantly. Following the description we indicate our recommendations for a sealer (if any) and floor finish.

Floor Finishes

There are two main categories of floor finishes: paste and liquid (emulsion) finishes. Paste wax can be used only on wood, linoleum, and cork floors. As applying and polishing paste waxes are so time-consuming, we assume you won't be using them and we'll have nothing more to say about those products.

An emulsion is just a stable mixture of liquids—in this case, water plus wax, or water plus plasticizers. If you see a reference to an emulsion on a product label, it means it is a water-based finish that can be spread easily with an applicator.

Emulsion finishes, in turn, are divided into waxes and polymers. The most prized of the waxes is carnauba because of its hardness. The waxes are reserved chiefly for wood floors and can be buffed to increase the gloss. The one we use is a commercial emulsion formula called Fortified Floor Wax.

Polymers are finishes that most closely resemble plastics or resins. Just about the only type of polymer you will hear about is an *acrylic* finish. Our Acrylic High-Gloss Floor Finish has a new commercial formula with a metal cross-link finish that is very hard and durable but that nevertheless can be stripped very easily. It can also be buffed to a higher gloss, unlike most acrylics.

In the sections that follow, when we use the term *wax* we will be referring to a liquid (emulsion) wax. The only type of polymer mentioned will be *acrylic*. And if we are referring to either type, we will use the general term *floor finish*.

RESILIENT FLOORS

"Resilient" means the ability of a material to resist shock or impact without permanent damage. A resilient floor is able to recover its thickness after a compressive force such as a heel has been applied to its surface. Resilient floors come in two forms: *sheets* up to 12 feet and *tiles* either 9 inches (asphalt) or 12 inches square.

Common types of residential resilient floors are vinyl (by far the most popular), polyurethane, and rubber. The lack of seams in sheet flooring makes it a practical choice for bathrooms, kitchens, laundry rooms, and entryways where water is likely to be spilled. Tiles are easy to install, but they must be laid snugly against each other to avoid gaps that can collect grunge and leak water to the subfloor. Paste waxes should *not* be used on any resilient floors except genuine linoleum. Acrylics are the preferred finish for all resilient floors except linoleum.

Because we recommend that resilient floors be treated differently depending on where they are in your house, these floors are listed below by room.

Kitchen Floors

The great majority of contemporary kitchen floors are resilient floors of vinyl ("wax" or "no-wax"), asphalt, or vinyl-composition material. If your floor isn't made of something else easily identifiable—like ceramic tile, quarry tile, wood, or marble—then it is almost certain to be one of the above. We recommend finishing all of these resilient kitchen floors (with the possible exception of no-wax floors—see below) with Acrylic High-Gloss Floor Finish. It is called a metal cross-link high-gloss acrylic. That's a mouthful, but it's worth the trouble. Its metal cross-link formula was one of the major breakthroughs in floor-maintenance chemistry in the past several years. It has an extremely durable finish that reduces the number of times you will have to refinish and, much more important, to strip the finish off again. Yet its chemical structure allows it to break its molecular bonds in response to floor strippers without putting up the fuss that most older waxes do. When you combine a metal cross-link finish with a no-rinse stripper, you have a state-of-the-art combination that cannot be surpassed in floor maintenance.

We also recommend that you seal all resilient kitchen floors before finishing them the first time (except the no-wax floors—see below). Also seal after the first time you strip the floor if you don't know if it had been sealed before. This is not a waste of your time even if it had, in fact, already been sealed. Applying an extra coat of sealer means you can usually get by with one less coat of finish. Besides, the sealer is typically cheaper than the finish, coat for coat. The type we use is a penetrating sealer (as opposed to a surface sealer) that can be used on all resilient floors except linoleum and cork. Those floors and wood floors call for a specialized wood sealer.

No-Wax Kitchen Floors

Well, there are two obvious choices with no-wax floors: (1) take their name literally and don't finish them; and (2) finish (protect) the floors anyway. We used to recommend, as did most others in this industry, that you treat no-wax floors with acrylic finish. This was because no-wax floors also need the protection that acrylics provide against normal wear and tear. But no-wax floors have improved in their durability in recent years, so you have a small decision to make at this point.

**So, do you finish no-wax
floors or not?**

No, as long as you're faithful about a regular maintenance schedule of sweeping or vacuuming, damp-mopping, and occasional washing. Needless to say, this choice is the faster of the two alternatives.

Yes, if you know in your heart of hearts that you aren't all that great about keeping the floor free of the grit and grime that will inevitably wear that nice, bright, new-looking floor finish into something less than that. Besides, does it still come as a surprise to you that "no-wax" floors may need finishing? After all, irons have settings for "permanent press" fabrics. Think about it.

For no-wax floors only, there is an alternative to acrylics that works well and is easier to maintain, because it doesn't build up and therefore doesn't require stripping. It is relatively new on the retail market and is called Bright (Johnson Wax Co.).

Whether you finish them or not, it's not necessary to seal these floors. A sealer will not provide any more protection than that built into the floor covering already.

Bathroom Floors

It doesn't matter what type of resilient flooring is in the bathroom. Don't finish it. Bathroom floors are exposed to too much moisture to be able to maintain a finished floor without extraordinary effort. Just keep it maintained during your normal cleaning routine. You may, however, apply a sealer if you prefer, and if your floor type allows for one. We recommend doing so only when the floor is new and if you are advised to do so by the manufacturer.

Laundry Rooms and Family Rooms

Follow the instructions for kitchen floors.

Entryways and Foyers

Finish and seal them as you would a standard kitchen floor. Finish them even if they are a no-wax floor. Even more important, make sure you have proper mats in these areas. Don't use rubber-backed mats on vinyl, vinyl composition, or asphalt flooring, as they may discolor the surface.

The following are the major classifications of resilient floors.

Vinyl sheet, inlaid. Particles of vinyl are compressed at high temperature into a thin, very hard layer, which is bonded to a backing material. The color runs all the way through the layer of vinyl. The vinyl is resistant to grease and oil, water, acids, detergents, and many solvents. It comes in "wax" or "no-wax" varieties. According to *Fine Homebuilding* magazine (August 1984), a good test for vinyl floor covering is to scratch a sample with your fingernail. If you come close to making a hole, forget it. A sealer and acrylic finish are recommended for this type of floor covering.

Vinyl sheet, rotogravure. If a resilient (spongy) layer is sandwiched between the vinyl and its backing, vinyl flooring becomes cushioned. A clear layer on top resists the wear. It is quieter to walk on than inlaid vinyl and comes in "wax" or "no-wax" varieties. The same fingernail test applies. Make sure the kind you purchase has a high-quality backing because a thin backing may allow nail heads to deform the surface eventually. A sealer and acrylic finish are recommended.

Linoleum sheet. Linoleum is a mixture of ground wood and cork, oxidized linseed oil, turpentine, resins, and pigments, all applied to a burlap or felt backing. It is vulnerable to alkalis such as ammonia and can require a sustained maintenance effort. Real linoleum hasn't been installed for years, so unless you have an older and unremodeled house, chances are slim that what's on your floor is linoleum. It may also be found as a countertop in older houses. It should have been sealed with a *wood* sealer and waxed with a liquid buffable floor wax designed for *wood* floors—not an acrylic finish.

Polyurethane sheet. This is a tough surface that requires little maintenance. Seal and finish it with an acrylic.

Vinyl composition tile. This is a blend of vinyl and other dense materials. It is slightly more vulnerable to household chemical attack than is solid vinyl tile, but has good resistance to grease and oil. Seal and finish it with an acrylic.

Vinyl tile. The surface is similar to inlaid vinyl sheet. Seal and finish it with an acrylic.

Rubber tile and sheet. This is made from synthetic and/or real rubber. It is durable, quiet, and waterproof but potentially horrendous to clean if textured. As it does not resist grease and oil, it's of questionable use in kitchens. It deteriorates in the presence of sunlight, so it cannot be installed in a porch or near an exterior window. Authorities do not recommend a sealer, but some specify two coats of acrylic.

Asphalt tile. This does not resist grease, fats, and oils because it is made from similar substances. Vinegar and fruit juice may soften and stain it if allowed to remain in contact for long. Obviously, it is not recommended for the kitchen. Liquid waxes, cleaners, or paste waxes with solvents must not be used or this floor will be damaged. As it can be similar in appearance to vinyl flooring, how can you tell the difference? The Cleaning Management Institute's test is to take a cloth and rub a small amount of lighter fluid or turpentine on a dark area of the floor. If the cloth picks up the dark color, the floor is asphalt. If not, its probably vinyl. Seal and finish asphalt tile with an acrylic.

Cork tile. This is made from the bark of the cork oak tree. The cork is ground up and then fused under heat and pressure. As it is the most comfortable and quiet of resilient floors, it's appropriate for hallways, libraries, and other rooms where peace is desired. But it performs badly if subjected to grease or oils or moisture, and must be sealed and waxed immediately after installation. Seal it with a *wood* sealer. Wax it with a finish suitable for a wood floor—either a liquid buffable floor wax or a paste wax (the latter if you have lots of time).

Ceramic and Quarry Tile Floors

The various types of ceramic tiles have in common that they are all baked clay. The finish may be *glazed* (gloss, satin, matte, or flat) and no sealer is required; or *unglazed* (no surface finish, usually earth tones), and it should be sealed. Quarry tile is a natural stone.

Glazed ceramic tiles themselves are impervious to most varieties of dirt. It's the grout that causes most of the cleaning problems. Whether or not the tile itself is sealed, we recommend that you seal the grout to make it easier to clean and more resistant to stains. Use a specialized grout sealer obtainable at a tile shop, a good hardware store, or through our catalog. Don't use steel wool on grouted tile floors: The steel-wool pads may shed tiny bits of steel that will get caught in the rough grout and rust. (For more information on sealing grout, see Chapter 13, "Prevention.")

The only time sealer is recommended for glazed tile is when the tile itself is very old and the glaze has been worn off. In that case, the tile becomes porous and very difficult to maintain. (One of the worst cleaning nightmares are floors made of thousands of small six-sided white tiles. Most of these floors are very old and exceedingly porous.) Seal such floors with a terrazzo sealer (two coats), but don't finish them. You may have to reseal the floor from time to time as the sealer is worn away.

Don't apply waxes or acrylics to the floors listed below. They are quite hard and don't need the protection of a finish coat. Also, omitting the finish coat will result in a less slippery floor—and these tiles do not need any encouragement in that direction.

Glazed tile. This comes in any of the four finishes (gloss, satin, matte, or flat), and smooth or textured surfaces. It includes small mosiac tiles sold in premounted sheets. Sealing is not required.

Patio tile. This tile is rough in texture and irregular in shape, and thicker than quarry or paver tiles. It must be sealed.

Paver tiles. These are large, usually unglazed, earth-tone tiles that must be sealed.

Quarry tile. This tile is rough in texture, usually unglazed red clay. Reddish terracotta tile (Italian for "baked earth") is just one color of quarry tile. If unglazed, use a terrazzo sealer followed by one or two optional coats of acrylic if a higher gloss is desired.

Masonry Floors

Marble. If you have marble floors in your house (villa?), you are probably in no doubt whatsoever that they are marble. You also probably have chilly feet if you walk around the house barefoot.

Marble floors require a specialized sealer obtainable from a janitorial supplier or a marble dealer. It may also be called a terrazzo sealer because the products are interchangeable. Avoid using steel wool on marble floors because tiny particles of steel left behind may rust. Marble floors are very vulnerable to any type of acid: orange juice, lemon juice, wine, vinegar, and so forth. If you have an acid spill, rinse immediately or else the marble will be etched and have to be resurfaced. If it is a serious spill, sprinkle baking soda on the area to neutralize the acid. Don't finish marble floors, but you may want to buff them for a higher gloss.

Terrazzo. *Terrazzo* is Italian for "terrace." It is made by embedding small pieces of marble in cement. The Portland cement matrix is vulnerable to spillage, so it should not be placed in kitchens or bathrooms or other areas subject to water damage. In houses, this type of floor is found mainly in outside steps and porches.

As terrazzo floors are mostly marble, treat them the same way that you would treat a marble floor.

Manufactured stone. These brick or concrete floors are extremely porous and irregular, so they will require several coats of both the sealer (two) and the finish coat (start with two).

Finish them with an acrylic.

Slate. Colors of slate include grays, greens, and blues. Slate floors will darken if sealed, so it is *not* often recommended unless you are willing to gamble with the several tons of stone installed as your floor. But you may want to finish them with an acrylic. Make sure that the finish does not make the slate slippery.

Flagstone floors. Seal these with penetrating masonry sealer, available from a tile shop. Finish with acrylic.

Wood Floors

Wood floors come in a variety of styles—stripwood, parquet, and plank being the most common. But for cleaning purposes, the primary consideration is the finish, not the style of installation.

Varathane (plastic) finishes. These days, most wood floors in the home are finished with varathane, polyurethane, or a similar plastic-like protective coating. If you have such floors—and this includes most install-it-yourself wood floors in the form of 12-inch by 12-inch squares—do *not* seal or finish them. The whole idea of plastic-like finishes was to spare you the necessity of all that work. They are superb treatments for wood floors and can last for a decade or more.

You may have noticed that our approach to wood floors is different from our approach to no-wax floors. We gave you a choice about whether or not to finish no-wax floors. In the case of a varathane finish, we recommend neither sealer nor an acrylic finish coat. It's relatively easy to strip the finish back off of no-wax floors, which you may have to do to insure additional protection of the finish. No such luck with wood floors; stripping them is difficult and hazardous both to the floor and to your lungs (because of the intensity of solvent strippers). Besides, you can add another coat of varathane in a few years to bring the shine back if necessary. You would have to replace a no-wax floor to accomplish the equivalent effect.

Varnish. Wood floors finished with varnish should be protected with both a sealer and a wax.

The sealer should be a penetrating sealer made for wood floors. Use either a paste wax (if you have all weekend) or a liquid buffable wax designed for wood floors like the Fortified Floor Wax we use. This product has carnauba wax suspended in a liquid vehicle. The carnauba wax provides its extra-hard protective finish that we've all heard about since we were kids. Because it's a liquid it can be applied with a wax applicator on a long handle, in vivid contrast to paste wax, which is applied on your hands and knees or with a floor machine. Needless to say, a quality liquid wax formulated for wood floors is our first choice.

The Floor You're Thinking About Installing

Designers, engineers, and architects who design the floors we walk on often seem to have abandoned us as far as cleaning is concerned. It's one thing for floors to be pretty, but they also need to be maintained for years to come. There are as many potential ways to finish, strip, and maintain floors as there are potential ideas for new floors. For example, whoever invented those beautiful-to-look-at textured rubber floors (you know, the ones that look like they have rubber quarters all over them) should be sentenced to clean those floors every day for the rest of his or her natural life. Cruel and unusual punishment? Indeed. But why stick us with them? They look great in the home for about an afternoon and dirty for the next ten or twenty years—unless, of course, you are willing to wash them on your hands and knees with a soft brush and to dry them thoroughly by hand with a cloth every single day.

When shopping for new floors, remember that highly *textured* resilient floors (including all those pretty, modern, no-wax ones with all their textured nooks and crannies) are not possible to maintain without spending far too much time and effort. You just can't stop dirt and wax and crud from setting up headquarters in all those little nooks and crannies and then resisting all but the most ingenious and time-consuming of methods to get them back out again. Possibly the worst offenders are textured resilient-tile floors that mimic ceramic-tile grout lines. *Grout!* Of all the things to imitate! Those fake grout lines are superb traps for an invincible wax buildup, dead raisins, grease spatters, and unidentifiable blobs of all sorts. One of the great pleasures of modern living? Hardly! Don't we all have better things to do with our time? If we quit buying these mistakes, maybe manufacturers will adequately field-test their products before unleashing them upon us.

Look for a floor that suits your taste and style but that is smooth—or nearly so. When you are deciding on a floor, talk seriously (to the salesperson, architect, designer, etc.) about how it is maintained. If they don't know, they shouldn't be selling the product. Period. And be sure you can easily lay your hands on the products they recommend before you make a final decision.

It's hard to believe how many phone calls we get from people asking how to clean, or what product to use, or whether to finish the floor they just had installed. They paid more than good money for it, but only after it was glued to the floor do they get around to asking someone how to take care of it for the next 10 or 15 years. Lousy timing—and all too often entirely too late to help.

8   STRIPPING FLOORS

Decisions

There are a few decisions to make before you strip wax from your floors: such as whether you should hire someone to do it, rent equipment to help you do it, or do it yourself by hand. But first, let's be sure we all agree what stripping wax off floors means and which specific floors we are talking about.

Wax

By "wax" we mean almost anything that has built up on your floors, no matter what the product is called. Some floor finishes are closer to liquid Saran Wrap than to real wax. "Miracle Floor Finish" this or "Super-Hard Long-Lasting" that are both varieties of what we're talking about. Even if the word *wax* isn't used in the name or printed on the product label, it still needs stripping if it's yellowed or unmanageable or unsightly.

Types of Floors

We are not going to spend much time with you figuring out what your floors are made of. We assume you just want the buildup off the floor and to get on with the weekend. The procedures described here for stripping floors apply almost exclusively to resilient floors such as vinyl sheet, vinyl tile, vinyl-asbestos, and so forth. The great majority of kitchen and bathroom floors fall into this category. (See Chapter 7, "Floor Coverings," for a more complete discussion.)

Precautions

Almost all contemporary floors will stand up reasonably well to the potentially harsh stripping process. You can*not* use this stripping procedure on wood or cork floors.

The fastest and safest stripping method for any floor is to use as little water as possible. Using less water also means that it will take less time to remove the water from the floor after you're done. It also minimizes possible damage to the floor—especially from leakage through the floor covering to the subfloor below. Even on nonporous, well-maintained floors, water can seep through cuts or other damaged areas, through seams between sheets of flooring, between tiles, along the walls, or in the corners. Buckling, delamination (separation of the flooring from the subfloor), and mold or dry rot can all be the result.

If you have a no-wax floor or a very shiny resilient floor, some scrub brushes can scratch the floor surface. Be sure to check before you really bear down on the floor with your brush, especially right in the middle (most visible) area. So test it in an inconspicuous place. If you can produce scratches with a brush, you'd better not use it. Use a sponge mop as much as possible. Resort to a white pad or a Kleenfast pad (in either case, always when the floor is wet) if the sponge mop is not strong enough.

Test Areas

Speaking of tests, you should also do a pretest of the stripper in a small, inconspicuous area of your floor (e.g., inside a closet or pantry) before you start sloshing it all over the place. A test area 6 inches square is just fine. The test will ease any fears about possible damage to the floors. You will also quickly discover if the stripper solution even works. Nice to know before you start work, because some of them don't!

Maybe you're unsure about whether your floors even need stripping. One very simple test is to apply stripper to a small area and see if the floor looks better. Usually the buildup is quite apparent. The floors will look uneven and yellowish or discolored. Unfortunately, it's not so easy to remove or ignore, especially when the in-laws are coming to visit.

Linoleum Floors

Most floors are safe for stripping, but there is one major exception. Stripped, older linoleum flooring (in either sheet or tile varieties) will often soften, and its colors will bleed. It appears to be melting—and it is! To test for this potential disaster, apply stripper to an out-of-the-way test area (6 inches by 6 inches is big enough) and remove the wax from this area. Rinse and dry. If you cannot achieve a satisfactory shine on the test area after applying a new coat or two of sealer and wax, stop what you're doing. You must not strip this floor. You'll just have to keep your floor clean and rewax it until you replace the floor or move out.

Bathroom Floors

If you have wax buildup on your bathroom floors, you shouldn't. Bathroom floors should not have been waxed. Bathroom floors are wet too often and washed too often for waxing to be a good idea. Once you've stripped the wax off this time, don't reapply any. Just keep the floor clean during regular maintenance cleaning (see our previous book, *Speed Cleaning*) and you'll be pleased with your decision not to rewax.

Hardwood Floors

The symptoms of wax buildup on hardwood floors are: floors are different in overall color (usually lighter in traffic areas), they have a blotchy surface and color (usually yellowish) in nontraffic areas, and bits of wax can be dug out with your fingernail. Even if you have all the symptoms, you must *not* strip wax from hardwood floors using any process that involves water. Water makes the grain of wood expand, potentially ruining the texture and causing edges to buckle. It's not possible to use water to remove wax without too great a risk of permanent damage to the floors.

Even though you can't strip this type of floor yourself, you don't have to live with it forever. Your choices are to refinish the floor or to call in a professional to strip the wax with a water-free solvent process using heavy-duty chemicals. If you're still intent on trying it yourself, check at a local janitorial supply store for a waterless stripper. We don't recommend it.

Hiring Someone to Strip the Floor

This is a job that you may want to hire someone else to do. The job can be a difficult and time-consuming one if there is much of a buildup. Also, wax is far easier to remove with professional equipment not found in most households: an electric floor machine to scrub down through the layers of wax and a wet/dry vacuum to pick up the spent stripper and wax *fast*.

Your decision should be based on how expensive it would be to have someone else do it versus how difficult the job will be for you. Perhaps most important, what are your alternatives for the weekend? If the wax buildup is truly demoralizing, you may want to have someone else do it this one time only, and then rewax it yourself. (See Chapter 9, "Waxing and Sealing Floors.") This will be the only time you'll ever have to spend money to hire someone else to strip the floor because it will never build up like this again if you follow our methods. If you do decide to hire someone, don't be surprised if you're charged by the hour and not by the job. It's often impossible to estimate how long a stripping job will take, especially if you don't know how many layers are on the floor. It's truly disheartening to spend all afternoon stripping a floor, only to find a subterranean layer just as tenacious as the first. And another . . . and another . . . and another . . .

Replacing the Floor Instead

This is absolutely the proper time to consider replacing the floor if it's close to being worn out or if you don't like it that much anyway. How much smarter to make this decision prior to stripping a badly built-up floor! You may be surprised how reasonable the cost of a new floor can be, especially the new seamless and groutless floors.

Choosing the Stripper

It's wise to use the stripper made by the same manufacturer as of the wax you intend to strip off because the stripper is formulated specifically to break down that wax. Otherwise, use a professional stripper such as the one we use, which requires no rinsing.

Preparing the Floor

It's a waste of time to wash the floor before you strip it. But do vacuum or sweep it first (if it needs it) to remove grit and debris that could later scratch the floor when it gets caught between the mop and the floor.

Before you start on the floor, take the time to move anything that will be in your way. If possible, move objects to countertops. If not, move them out of the room. If you have a freestanding piece of furniture in an area that needs stripping, you must move it out of the room. Now is also the time to move little items like the dog and cat dishes. Don't wait until your hands are wet and slippery and you can't get a good grip on anything. *Clear the decks.*

METHOD ONE — BY HAND

MATERIALS

Here are the supplies you'll need if you're going to do this job by hand—that is, without renting a floor machine or wet/dry vacuum. If you are planning on renting such equipment, skip ahead to *Method Two.*

   wax stripper
 1 double bucket or two single buckets
 1 mop with scrub-brush attachment or scrub brush on a long handle
 1 Kleenfast pad, handle, and extra pads
   several white scrub pad/sponges
 ½ package of coarse (#2) steel wool
 1 plastic dustpan
 1 spray bottle of Red Juice
10 cleaning cloths
 1 cleaning apron
 1 toothbrush
 1 scraper
 1 cleaning tray
 1 pair of rubber gloves
 1 floor squeegee

Getting Dressed

Tie your apron snugly around your waist. Be sure the scraper and toothbrush are in their respective pockets. Take four or five cleaning cloths and put them in an apron pocket. Also take a white pad and a steel wool pad and put them in a plastic-lined apron pocket. If you have a hand-held Kleenfast pad instead of one at the end of a handle, put it an apron pocket. Hang the Red Juice on its proper apron hook. Take the stripper and the bucket to the sink to mix the proper concentration of stripper.

The Starting Point

Follow label instructions for diluting the stripper. Don't use full strength unless instructed to do so. Be sure to do a small, inconspicuous test area the first time you do this job or when you change brands of stripper. Put the stripper and (usually warm) water solution in one side of the double bucket. Put the squeegee, dustpan, and scrub-brush attachment in the empty side of the bucket. Grab your mop and Kleenfast pad and move to the left-hand corner farthest from the exit doorway.

The Strategy

The secrets to stripping the floor quickly are to work section by section and always to have a coat of stripper softening the wax in a section *in advance* of the section you are scrubbing. The idea here is to let the chemicals in the stripper loosen up the wax buildup so *you* don't have to. Apply a coat of stripper to Section 1 and Section 2 (see schematic on p. 99). Then scrub and remove the wax from Section 1. Before you start scrubbing Section 2, apply more stripper in Section 3. The Section 3 stripper will be softening wax while you scrub Section 2, and so forth. That's the general idea. Now let's get more specific.

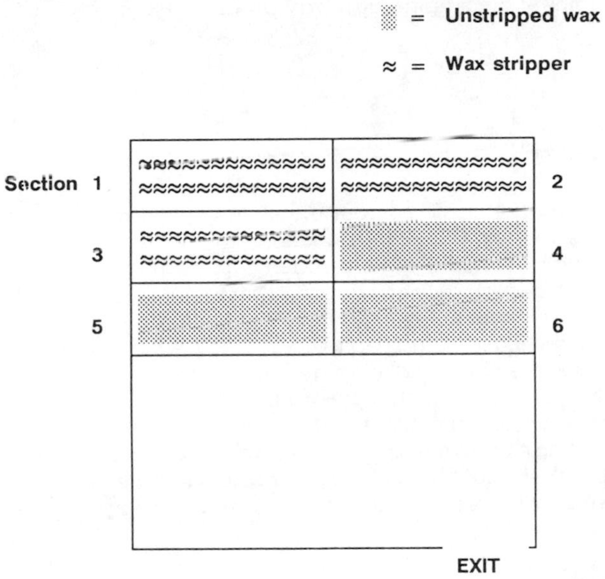

= Unstripped wax

≈ = Wax stripper

Section 1

2

3

4

5

6

EXIT

Change the pattern of the sections as necessary to avoid having to walk in stripper or on already finished sections as you approach the exit. When you get to the last section, park the equipment outside the doorway on newspaper or rags to protect the adjacent floor.

Applying the Stripper Solution

Starting in the left-hand corner farthest from the exit, use the mop liberally to wet a section approximately 2 feet by 4 feet. (Don't follow any label instruction that says 3 feet by 3 feet because you won't be able to reach a problem spot that needs hand-scrubbing on the far side of such a deep square.) Don't make a flood that may loosen the floor covering, but at the same time don't be stingy with the stripper—especially in the corners and along the baseboards and other areas where you can see heavy wax. The idea is to get the floor wet enough that it won't dry out before you're finished. You'll quickly learn how much is needed.

As soon as the stripper comes in contact with the wax it starts its chemical attack to soften it. Instead of wasting time waiting while this chemical action takes place, move to the right and wet another 2-foot by 4-foot section. Notice if there is any wax on the baseboards and remember to wet them also when you first apply stripper.

The Scrub Brush

Next you'll need a scrub brush or its equivalent to scrub the wax loose. If you're using our mop, you can just exchange the sponge mop head for the scrub-brush attachment. This may not be all that simple, however, because the sponge is wet and slippery. An extra pole for the brush costs only a few dollars and allows you to avoid having to switch tools back and forth on the same mop handle. If you find that you can apply the stripper satisfactorily with the brush, then you can eliminate the mop altogether and just use the brush for both application and scrubbing.

The scrub-brush attachment to the mop should be right there in the dry side of the double bucket. If you're not using our mop and its attachment, use a Kleenfast pad or stiff-bristled brush on a long handle to scrub with. The other choice is to work on your hands and knees with a hand-held brush or white pad. So now, starting in Section 1, use whatever tool you have chosen to finish loosening up the wax.

Scrapers, Steel Wool, and Scrub Pads

Use your scraper on heavily built-up areas—like along the wall and in the corners. Use it carefully, always on a wet floor, and at a low angle.

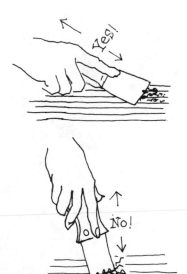

You can also very carefully use the corner of the scraper to remove wax from dents in the tile. (Remember when you dropped the iron point-first into the floor, just missing your foot?)

It can be tricky avoiding making scratches when using the scraper. Less troublesome are white pads, steel wool, or a Kleenfast pad. Because these items don't cost much, we like to have them all available to select which one works best for the particular wax and floor. You'll soon choose your favorites and replace them only when they're worn out. Start with a scrub brush or Kleenfast pad. Then move up to a white pad or steel wool or scraper if necessary. (Rule 7: Shift to a heavier-duty tool.) Careful: Steel wool should not be used on marble or grouted tile floors because tiny bits of steel may become lodged in floor crevices and rust.

Don't drive yourself crazy if a section doesn't respond after a reasonable effort. You may be dealing with layer upon layer of wax. If a section is really stubborn, stop messing with it mechanically. Rather, remove the wax residue, reapply some stripper to the area, and move on. (Don't worry, we won't forget about it.)

Adjusting the Size of the Cleaning Sections

It is important that you not let the floors dry before you've finished scrubbing. But it wastes time to put on more water than you need because you'll just have to remove the excess. So if the floor is getting dry before you finish a section, use a little more stripper solution and/or reduce the size of each section to 2 feet by 3 feet next time. Conversely, if you're having no problems with a section getting dry before you finish it, then you might increase the size to 2 feet by 5 feet. The idea is to make the section as large as you can and yet still be able to finish before the stripper gets dry. This speeds up the job and reduces the time you'll need to finish with this mess.

Baseboards

Previous waxers have often inadvertently waxed the baseboards an inch or two up from the floor. If that's the case, you must remove that accumulation also (and don't reapply it!). Use your Kleenfast pad, white pad, and/or steel wool here.

Don't forget to wipe this wax residue off the baseboards with a cleaning cloth after you remove the residue from each section of the floor next to the baseboard.

Removing the Wax

Once you've loosened the wax—at least most of it—in a 2-foot by 4-foot section, the next step is to remove the fine mess you've made out of water, stripper, partially liquefied wax, grease, dirt, and whatever else was on your floor. Use a squeegee and a plastic dustpan. You can use your prized window-washing squeegee for this task if you plan on replacing the rubber blade with a new one when you finish. Otherwise, use a specialized heavy-duty floor squeegee.

Use the squeegee to pull the waxy mess toward you, to the right, and into the dustpan. Then dump the contents of the dustpan into the empty half of the double bucket. This keeps the stripper solution clean so it lasts longer. Furthermore, you won't have to run back and forth to the sink to pour out the muck you'd get if you mixed the wax residue with the fresh stripper solution. Alternatively, use two separate buckets (one for stripper and one for the gunk).

If the wax residue on the floor is so watery that the squeegee and dustpan aren't effective, use a sponge mop and add clean rinse water to the empty half of the bucket. Squeeze the residue from the mop into the rinse water and use it to rinse the mop.

When the stripper is removed (using either the squeegee and dustpan or the sponge mop), apply stripper to the next 2-foot by 4-foot section (Section 3). In most cases, locate it next to Section 2 (see the illustration). Do this *before* you scrub Section 2—where the wax by now is mostly softened.

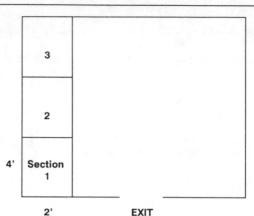

Back to Those Problem Spots Again

Let's say you had to leave behind problem spots in Section 1 that still had some stubborn unstripped wax, and they are now soaking in stripping solution again. Your strategy will be a bit different than if there were no such pockets of resistance. To minimize the number of times you traipse back and forth through wet stripper, it may be best to go to the opposite side of the room for the next section in which to apply stripper (see the illustration). So now presoak Section 3 with stripper. Let the earlier problem spots continue to soak until you are done scrubbing and squeegeeing Section 2. Then go back and finish them before going any farther. This strategy works best in a large room. If it's small, do the best you can to stay out of your own way. If you are having persistent problems removing all the wax, use the stripper full strength (undiluted with water).

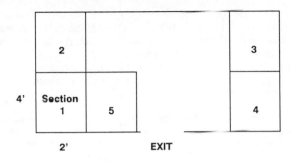

Even if you follow these directions carefully, you may still have to walk over a section you've already stripped or one that's still covered with stripper. Just be careful of the slippery areas, and don't track stripper into sections that you've finished. To avoid tracking the stripper use a few cloths to make a path, and step on the cloths instead of on the floor.

Removing the Last of the Stripper

You'll save the most time if you use a no-rinse stripper. If you use a standard stripper that requires rinsing, be sure to thoroughly rinse the floor after you've finished stripping it because any remaining stripper will react with the wax you're about to apply. This is a time-consuming extra step, of course, requiring extra trips back and forth to the sink that could have been avoided.

When using a no-rinse stripper, be certain to remove all the stripper solution. This isn't all that hard to do. Squeegee carefully and move the little bit of stripper solution that's left over each time into the next section you haven't scrubbed yet. For example, squeegee all the spent solution you can from Section 1 into the dustpan and pour it into the bucket. Then squeegee into Section 2 the remaining little bit of stripper solution that isn't easy to pick up. This way, you'll only have to fuss with the last trace of solution once (in the very last section you do). Then use a cleaning cloth to pick it up.

When you run out of stripper solution and/or finish the floor, dump both sides of the double bucket into a sink or toilet. Make sure it's all rinsed from the sink and flushed completely down the drain with plenty of hot water. Also, rinse out both sides of the bucket so you don't end up with wax buildup there too!

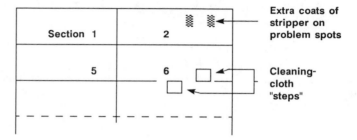

Review

Remember, the secret to stripping the floor as quickly and painlessly as possible is always to have stripper soaking the section ahead of where you are currently working so it loosens the wax before you get there. The same principle holds true for the problem spots. When they resist your efforts on the first attempt, don't spin your wheels (let alone work up a sweat and waste time). Rather, squeegee the whole section, apply more stripper solution on the problem spots, and move on to the next section. Scrub the next section and return to the previous problem spots before moving on. If they still don't come around after scrubbing a second time, repeat the process by rewetting with stripper and returning once more.

What Next?

Unless you have decided not to rewax, you should be prepared to apply the wax as soon as the floor dries, or no later than the next morning. (See Chapter 9, "Waxing and Sealing Floors.") The floor is now nice and clean and you wouldn't want to wait for it to get dirty before you wax it. To speed drying time, you can aim a room fan across the floor. The air moving over the surface speeds drying time significantly. Heating the room helps, too, of course.

**METHOD TWO — USING A FLOOR MACHINE
AND WET/DRY VAC**

You may want to be kind to yourself and rent a floor machine and a wet/dry vacuum to assist you in stripping a floor. We heartily recommend this method if you have a large room to strip or if the wax buildup is severe. The floor machine can do double duty as a carpet cleaner (see Chapter 10, "Cleaning Carpets"), and the wet/dry vac will save an amazing amount of time, and wear and tear on your back. Both of them are available at most equipment-rental stores.

A floor machine can be difficult for some people to manage. Unless you're someone who is not intimidated by such mechanical challenges, don't even try it. When considering whether or not to rent machinery, also weigh the time involved to drive to and from the rental place (*twice*) and the extra cost in relation to the size of your floor.

If you do rent the equipment, get both machines (or, better yet, buy your own wet/dry vacuum and just rent the floor machine). There's nothing stopping you, of course, from combining features of Methods 1 and 2. For example, if you don't want to tangle with the floor machine, you might want to scrub with a brush by hand but pick up the stripper solution with a wet/dry vac. Or you could power-scrub with the floor machine but pick up the stripper solution with a floor squeequee and dustpan.

MATERIALS

Here are the materials you'll need if you've decided to strip the floor with the aid of a floor machine and a wet/dry vacuum.

```
   wax stripper
 1 double bucket or two single buckets
 1 mop
 1 Kleenfast pad and handle
 3 white scrub pad/sponges
½ package coarse (#2) steel wool
 1 spray bottle of Red Juice
10 cleaning cloths
 1 cleaning apron
 1 toothbrush
 1 scraper
 1 cleaning tray
 1 pair of rubber gloves
 1 wet/dry vacuum
 1 floor machine: 17-inch diameter or smaller, plus stripping pads
```

Floor Machine

The floor machine suitable for use at home is one that has a single rotating disc powered by a motor that sits directly above it. The disc is a brush with firm nylon bristles, but they're not for use directly on the floor. Rather, the bristles hold in place plastic pads of varying roughness that do the stripping, scrubbing, and polishing that the machine is capable of.

For our purposes, the floor machine works by scrubbing the wax off the floor with a high-speed rotating stripping pad (usually red or black) that is pressed firmly against the floor by the weight of the machine itself. The stripping pad is the same diameter as the brush and is made of a modern abrasive substance much like the white scrubbing pad we use. Pads come with the floor machine when you rent it. Be sure to explain to the salesperson what you are using the machine for, so he or she can determine what type of pad you need. (Different pads are used for polishing, applying wax, etc.)

Like the white pad, the stripping pad wears out after some use, so be sure to bring enough of them home so you won't run out halfway through the job. It's no fun to have to make a *third* trip to the rental store to get one more stripping pad! We suggest that you take a few more than the store personnel recommend and, of course, return the unused ones for credit when you return the floor machine.

Rent a machine whose disc is 17 inches or less in diameter. Insist that the salesperson give you a demonstration or good instructions on how to operate and control it. The machine is easy to handle only *after* you know how. Otherwise it will seem impossible to manage and it can easily result in torn (or very tired) muscles and/or damage to your baseboards or furniture.

Operating the Floor Machine

The secret to using a floor machine is to control its movement and direction by slightly raising or lowering its handle—*not* by twisting the handle or by brute force. This *slight* change makes the clockwise-rotating brush dig into the floor a little bit more in the front or back. The machine will move to the right (up) or the left (down), depending on this change in friction. If you don't follow these directions, your first impulse will be to try to change the direction of the machine by brute force, which even a very strong

person can barely accomplish. Force won't stop the machine fast enough from going where it wants to go. For example, it may want to remove one leg of the piano—which is then not supported by the others. Accidents occur. Strong men whimper. Pets run for cover. Terror stalks the hallways of your home. However, once you try the simple up-and-down approach with the handle, a floor machine is something of a pussycat to operate.

For the well-being of your back, it is important to find a comfortable level at which to hold the floor-machine handle—usually just below the waist. Too high and you will wear out your arms and shoulders. Too low and you will feel emergency messages from your vertebrae. The best way to manage the long cord is to put it over one shoulder when the machine is operating, so wear an old shirt or blouse that you won't mind getting dirty. Wear old tennis shoes or other nonslip shoes you can afford to ruin. You need good traction while doing this wet work.

Getting Dressed

Tie your apron snugly around your waist. Be sure the scraper and toothbrush are in their respective pockets. Take four or five cleaning cloths and put them in an apron pocket. Also take a white pad and a steel-wool pad and put them in a plastic-lined apron pocket. If you have a hand-held Kleenfast pad, put it in an apron pocket. Hang the Red Juice on its proper apron hook. Take the stripper and the bucket to the sink to mix the proper concentration of stripper.

Getting Started

Follow label instructions for diluting the stripper. Don't use full strength unless instructed to do so. Be sure to do a small, inconspicuous test area the first time you do this job or when you change brands of stripper. Put the stripper and (usually warm) water solution in one side of the double bucket. Move to the left-hand corner farthest from the exit doorway.

With a sponge mop, apply the stripper solution to two adjacent sections approximately 3 feet by 6 feet. Keep two such sections covered with stripper at all times. The first is the one you're scrubbing with the floor machine. The second has the stripper, presoftening the wax for easier removal when you get to it with the floor machine. Apply enough solution to this second section so it doesn't dry out before you get to it. If you do have this problem, then reduce the size of each section to 3 feet by 4 feet. On the other hand, if you're having no problem managing the 3-feet by 6-feet sections, go ahead and make them a bit larger. The fewer and larger the sections, the faster the job will go. Keep moving the bucket so it is positioned where you'll need it next *and* where it will be out of your way.

Depending on the shape of your room, there are several ways to proceed. Here are two examples: (1) For square rooms, start in the far left corner and work to the right. When you come to a corner, go back to the left wall, move out 3 feet, and work back toward the right. (2) For narrow rooms or rooms with an exit in the middle, it may be faster to alternate from one end of the room to the other. (See illustration.)

Corners and Baseboards

You must clean the corners by hand because the floor machine's circular brushes won't reach into them. Carry a white scrub pad, steel wool (except for marble and grouted floors), or a hand-held Kleenfast pad in your apron pocket for the corners and other places you'll need to get at by hand. The same is true with baseboards if previous waxers have splashed them with wax. If so, be sure to coat the baseboards with stripper when you are applying it to the floor. Be liberal with the stripper in the corners and anywhere else the buildup is heaviest.

Maneuver the machine carefully along the walls. It will splash wax and stripper onto the baseboards (in addition to the stripper you have already applied there). Use

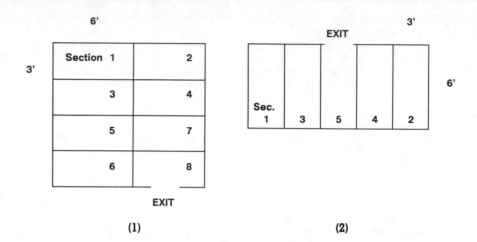

(1)   (2)

a cleaning cloth to wipe the baseboards to remove the wax that was there and any stripper the machine has deposited. The time to wipe the baseboards is when you use the wet/dry vac (or squeegee) to remove the mess on the floor. Wipe them while they're within reach. If you wipe the baseboards too soon, you'll just get them dirty again when you bring the floor machine close to that area. If you wait too long, you already know what will happen—fossilized floor wax.

This is an important step because if the baseboards redry, the wax and dirt from the floor will be just as hard to remove from them as they were from the floor—except that it is even uglier on the baseboards because it's now lumpy and dirty and disgusting. If the stripper mixture manages to become dry and hard by the time you get to it, dip a white pad into the stripper solution and try again. The stripper will soften the gunk and make it easy to wipe clean.

Wet/Dry Vacuums

The wet/dry vacuum (sometimes called a shop vacuum) is easy to operate and maneuver. It's a logical and reasonable item to purchase for many homes. In addition to stripping and cleaning floors, it can be used for wet-cleaning carpets and upholstery and vacuuming the garage or patio or porch. It's a life-saver for the occasional household flood (acts of nature or otherwise). But don't buy the cheapest model because it won't pick up enough water to be helpful.

Picking Up the Mess

During floor stripping, the time to use the wet vac is after you've finished scrubbing each 3-foot by 6-foot section with the floor machine. Let's take a square room as an example (see the illustration on p. 114). Scrub Section 1 with the floor machine and leave it at the closest corner of Section 2. Use the wet vac to remove all traces of the stripper solution from Section 1.

When you've vacuumed up all traces of Stripper in Section 1, park the wet vac behind your bucket. Apply stripper to Section 3. Then strip Section 2, and so forth until done. The idea is to relocate equipment to a spot as close as possible to the area in which you will use it next—without putting it in your own way.

Stubborn Spots

Don't be afraid to add more stripper to Section 1 if you find that it's not thoroughly stripped of wax. In fact, that's the correct way to get the job over as quickly as possible. When a section doesn't come clean after your first effort, don't scrub it again just yet. Rather, apply more stripper where needed to continue the chemical battle and then move on to scrub the next section. Then, after you've finished scrubbing that

```
┌──────────────┬──────────────────┐
│              │                  │
│  Section 1   │  Section 2       │    --The floor machine
│              │  x Floor Machine │       is INSIDE
│              │                  │       Section 2 .
├──────────────┤                  │
│              │  x Wet Vac       │
│  Section 3   │                  │
│              ├──────────────────┤
│              │  x Mop & Bucket  │    --The mop and bucket
│              │                  │       are OUTSIDE
│              │                  │       future Section 4 .
│              │                  │
│              │                  │
│              │                  │
│              │                  │
└──────────────┴──────────────────┘
                 EXIT
```

This illustration shows the state of affairs just after you finish scrubbing and wet-vacuuming Section 1. You had already applied stripper to Section 2, and the floor machine was left in Section 2 to use there next. The wet vac stands nearby, ready for use as soon as you finish with the floor machine in Section 2.

section, apply stripper to the next section and return the machine to the problem spots in the original section for another go at them. But finish the problem spots before you get so far away that you have to drag the machine over places you have already stripped and wet-vacuumed dry. As shown in the illustration, if you have problem spots in Section 1, reapply stripper to them and move on to Section 2. After you finish Section 2, just be sure to return to Section 1 to finish up there before you move on to scrub Section 3.

Reach for one of your hand-scrubbing tools (steel wool, white pad, or Kleenfast pad) as needed when you're wet-vacuuming and discover you've missed a few small spots. That way you won't have to bring back the floor machine unnecessarily. Your bucket is nearby for additional stripper if you need it, but usually you can do it with just the pad because the wax is already softened.

Black Heel Marks

If encountered while stripping, rub out with the steel wool or a scrub pad, wet with a little stripper. According to the Cleaning Management Institute, the main cause of black heel marks is an insufficient finish on the floor. Without an adequate finish, heels rub on the floor with a greater resistance and tend to mark more easily. This is not to say that you should apply a thicker finish coat. Rather, if you're getting an abundance of such marks you might check to see if the floor finish has been worn away and if it's time to refinish the floor.

What Next?

You should be prepared to go ahead and seal and/or wax the room now because the floor is nice and clean. Who knows how long it will stay that way? If it does get dirty, you will just have to wash it again before you apply wax. (See Chapter 9, "Waxing and Sealing Floors.")

9   WAXING AND SEALING FLOORS

The first decision to be made is whether your particular floor should be waxed or not. Hand in hand is the decision of whether or not to seal it. And you'll need to know what products to use. If you're familiar with your floor and have already made these decisions, we're ready to get right to it. If you have questions about what type of covering your floor has and whether or not it needs waxing and/or sealing, first check Chapter 7, "Floor Coverings."

Although we recognize that some floor coverings require waxes and others require acrylics (Chapter 7), for the sake of brevity we'll refer to all finishes as "waxes" in this chapter. Likewise, as the procedures are the same for applying sealer or wax, we'll refer to sealers as "waxes" also. If your particular floor requires a sealer, apply it before the wax, of course, but in exactly the same way.

Condition of the Floor

Now that the hard job of stripping the floor is out of the way (it *is* out of the way, right?), and as stripping leaves the floor nice and clean, you can now proceed directly to the easier part—applying the wax. Otherwise, make sure the floor is absolutely clean before you wax it. So if it needs it, wash it now and rinse it thoroughly before applying wax. Use clear ammonia (3 to 4 tablespoons) and water on all your floors—including varathane-finished wood floors (but *not* bare or waxed wood floors). Rinse the floor twice. The reason for the extra rinse is that alkalis or other harsh agents in liquid cleaners can react poorly with the floor wax. One of the unfortunate results is "flashing," or irregular spots of dull wax. Because residual alkalis can make it impossible to get a high shine, rinse with care so your finished work will look as nice as possible after all your effort.

Now the floor is sparkling clean from your stripping or cleaning job. If it isn't, every little piece of fuzz, every single hair, every crumb of every cracker left on the floor will be enshrined in the wax for you to see every time you enter the room until it's time to strip and rewax again. So be sure the floor is clean.

Despite all the advertising hoopla, we have found that how you prepare the floor and how you apply the product are more important than the product itself. Correct preparation and application allow you to get the maximum benefits from the floor finish—in degree of protection, appearance, and duration of coverage. Besides a great-looking floor, you'll also create a lot of free time that you would otherwise have wasted by doing the floor improperly or inefficiently and by having to repeat the whole process in three months instead of in six to twelve.

MATERIALS

Stock your cleaning tray with the following items:

    10 cleaning cloths
     1 spray bottle of Red Juice
     1 white scrub pad/sponge combination ("white pad")
     2 pads of 0000 steel wool
     1 pair of rubber gloves
       sealer—depends on type of floor (see Chapter 7, "Floor Coverings")
       floor finish—depends on type of floor (see Chapter 7 "Floor Coverings")

Stock your Speed Clean apron with:

     1 toothbrush
     1 scraper
     2 plastic bags (as liners) with clips

Hand-carry the following:

     1 fake lambswool wax applicator with a long handle

This chapter is designed to teach you step-by-step techniques of how to get waxing over within as short a time as possible and to free you from repeating the process for a very long time.

The Starting Point

Set your cleaning tray just outside the doorway through which you will eventually exit. Take your apron and tie it around your waist snugly, Check to be sure that the toothbrush and scraper are in their proper pockets. Hang the Red Juice on the side of your apron on which you usually carry it. Put four or five cleaning cloths in an apron pocket. Stuff the white pad and a steel-wool pad into a plastic-lined pocket. Hand-carry the wax applicator and the wax to the far left corner of the room away from the door you'll eventually exit through.

Setting Up

One of the things that makes this job so much easier to experienced professionals is that they take the time to *first* move anything that may eventually be in the way. Move any furniture that you can completely out of the room—not just across the room, where it will be out of the way only half of the time. Likewise, remove the smaller things—like the little trash can in the corner that you would otherwise trip over sooner or later, spilling half the wax and tipping the garbage into the wet wax. Take the time to tie up the drapes or curtains if they will hang in the path of the wax applicator. Do it now, not when you are right in the middle of the job and have to stop everything to find a string or coat hanger. This little preventive step may seem annoying, but the alternative is to end up with wax on your curtains forever more. Close the doors to nearby rooms if dust is going to blow in from them. Oh, and put the dog and cat out. You're on your own with your kids.

Now you can move around the room unimpeded instead of tripping over things, wrestling with the curtains, having the dog chase the cat through the wax, or tripping and spilling wax. Why *ask* for trouble?

Convenience and safety aren't the only reasons professionals move everything out of the way. It's also the fastest way to get this job done. They will have the time to do another job. You will have the time to finish this job and still go on a picnic while it dries.

Strategy

The most important strategy to observe while applying wax is to spread the wax perfectly evenly in as *thin* a layer as humanly possible. A thin layer will give you the most beautiful appearance, the maximum protection and duration, and the easiest removal later if necessary. Two or three very thin coats look much better than one thick coat no matter how carefully the thick coat is applied. Too heavy a coat will make a floor dull, will increase the ability of the wax to trap dirt, and may alter the apparent color of the floor. A very thick coat may harden on the top but stay soft underneath permanently, which causes all sorts of maintenance problems and can make the floor slippery.

Using the Wax Applicator

First of all, use a wax applicator. The one we use costs about four bucks. Your knees are worth at least that much—or more. Each. Second, use a brand-new fake disposable lambswool pad in the applicator—or at least one that was very well washed out the last time you used it and doesn't feel hard or stiff like an old paintbrush. Wet the applicator with water and wring it as dry as you can, then install it on the applicator.

Starting in the left corner farthest from the exit, pour a small amount (about ½ cup) of wax directly onto the floor. Don't pour it all in one spot. Instead, squirt the wax in 3-foot lines from one end of the area to the other and back again. This makes a kind of long skinny oblong. Hold the bottle low to the floor so you aren't splashing wax all over. Use the wax applicator to spread the wax over an area of the floor about 3 feet by 3 feet.

The best way to evenly distribute the wax is to make back-and-forth motions with the wax applicator from one end of the 3-foot by 3-foot square to the other and then back again. You don't have to step forward and back to do this—just a couple of side steps to get from one end to the other. If you do it this way, it's almost impossible to end up with puddles or thick areas of wax or missed spots. Just don't put too much wax on the floor to begin with. Remember, the ideal is one molecule thick, not ¼ inch!

Do be alert as you move your applicator back and forth not to miss small spots. They will stand out later as prominently as the spots you miss on your car when washing it.

If you don't follow our directions, one of the results may be bubbles in the wax generated by the wax applicator. The way to avoid this is to spread the wax out without going back and forth over the same area repeatedly with the wax applicator. Don't *scrub* with the applicator. It's not a mop. Your goal is just to smooth out the liquid over the surface. Two back-and-forth motions with the applicator should do.

Pouring the wax in small quantities does seem to slow you down, but the results are so much better that it's eminently worth the effort. You are only going to apply this finish a couple of times a year but you will have to look at it a few thousand times a year, so it makes sense to be very exacting during this application stage.

All the usual rules and exhortations apply for protecting your back. If you have a back problem, I'm sure you're well aware of it. Use the applicator while standing as erect as possible. Bend your legs, not your back, especially while pouring wax from the container onto the floor.

Working Your Way Around the Room

After you complete the first 3-foot by 3-foot area, move to the right and repeat the process. It you are proceeding properly, the previous area will still be damp and the wax from the new and old areas will blend together easily. But be attentive when you join two such areas together as it is easy to miss a little bit of floor here. Progress from area to area across the room to the right. Just step back and start across the room in the other direction when you finish your first row. Repeat the process until you've done the entire floor. Remember, the method is the same whether you are applying sealer or wax.

Dirt in the Wax Applicator

If your wax applicator gets dirty, it shouldn't. Your floor should be so clean that the applicator looks wet only, not particularly dirty. If it does get dirty, stop and rinse it clean before proceeding further. Repeat if necessary because once it gets dirty it will start applying some of that dirt back onto the floor mixed in with the wax. There is no need to clean the applicator pad when switching from sealer to wax.

Little Mystery Globs

If, while you're applying wax, you come across mystery matter still on the floor, grab a tool and remove it before proceeding. Use your scraper on larger masses and the toothbrush, white pad, or steel-wool pad (except on marble or grouted floors) on smaller bits of previously missed matter. Deposit the remains in the plastic-lined debris pocket of the apron so it doesn't end up immortalized in the wax. If necessary, use a little Red Juice to help pick up the more stubborn pockets of resistance. But be sure to wipe any such areas completely dry before you apply any wax because there's no telling how Red Juice or any other cleaner will react with the wax. Use a cleaning cloth from your apron to do this.

How Many Coats?

If you're applying both a sealer and a wax, we recommend two coats of each. It doesn't take long to let the first coat of sealer dry completely—everywhere in the room—before applying another thin coat. One coat of sealer may look great, but go ahead with the second coat to maximize protection and appearance. The goal is not to have to do this again for a long, long time.

As with the sealer, even if one coat of wax looks just fine, go ahead and apply the second coat. You want the layers of wax to absorb the wear and tear without breaking through to the sealer. Again, be sure to let each coat dry completely before starting the next one.

If you're having trouble getting the floors to dry between coats, a couple of procedures can help. The first, as you might have guessed, is to keep the heat on in the room if it's chilly. Not too hot, mind you, or you'll have a hard time working in the room. The second is to aim a room fan across the floor surface. Moving air will dry the surface much more quickly. Just be careful that the fan doesn't suck in all sorts of debris from the next room. As long as you apply the wax in very thin coats, it should dry quite quickly. If your floor isn't dry within 20 minutes you are probably applying it too thickly.

Avoiding Wax Buildup

You can really do yourself a favor by applying wax correctly in the first place so you don't create removal problems for yourself later on. The main reason for wax buildup (other than applying it too often and too thick) is applying wax to areas where it doesn't get worn off by foot traffic. You may have noticed, when you were stripping the floor, that the worst wax buildup was near the walls and in the corners—where there is little foot traffic. There was little or no wax to strip off from the more traveled areas of the room, where the wax is continually worn off by foot traffic. As it is almost impossible to walk closer to the wall than 6 inches, any wax applied there will never get worn off. It will remain there unscathed indefinitely.

Here's a rule to avoid wax buildup during application: Apply both coats of sealer and the first coat of wax all the way to the baseboard. But do not apply the second coat of wax any closer than *6 inches* from the baseboard or wall. Also do not apply successive coats—even months later—any closer than 6 inches from the baseboard. This wax-free zone also includes any other places that don't get heavy traffic—like small strips of floor between appliances, or a large corner area that gets little traffic, or under a work island, and so forth. You should be able to recall which areas of your room aren't walked on much if you are the one who had the pleasure of stripping the wax off the floor. The places where the wax buildup was the worst are the same ones to avoid applying a second coat of wax. Even if you didn't strip your floor, take the time to think it over. Don't ignore this rule and routinely apply wax to the entire floor. Not only does overwaxing cause removal problems later on, but also it starts to make the floor look worse and worse.

Cleanup

When you are finished with the final coat of wax, either throw away the fake lambswool pad or clean it. We recommend that you just toss it. It's inexpensive, and washing it completely free of wax and sealer is something of an ordeal—especially after you've just worked your floor over three or four times. Washing it is a bit like trying to get all the paint out of a paint roller. But if you do want to save it, rinse it very well with water to prevent it from hardening as it dries. After it dries completely, store it in a sealed plastic or paper bag to prevent it from accumulating debris in storage. If you wait until the wax dries before you try to clean it, you may find it impossible to do.

Be patient and let the floor dry thoroughly before you try to replace the furniture and other items that you originally moved out of the way. To avoid temptation, it helps to have made plans to be out of the house (treat yourself to something) to let the floor completely dry. It's a shame to move furniture and other items back into the room only to discover that part of the floor wasn't quite dry. You don't want to have to try to figure out how to fix an area—or to have to ignore it and have your footprints immortalized in the wax. This point is really a version of Rule 5—"Don't rinse before it's clean."

Congratulations! If you've followed the directions faithfully, you have just sealed and waxed your floor like a pro. Your floor will look better than it has since it was installed, and it will give you satisfaction a long time before you'll have to rewax.

Rewaxing

As we said, don't apply wax close to walls, corners, or nontraffic areas after the first coat, no matter how long it has been between coats. Wash and rinse the floor well, and apply wax only to the traffic areas of the floor. It doesn't matter that the new and old areas temporarily appear different when you're applying the wax, or that it's so easy to apply the wax right up to the baseboards. Don't do it! The visible difference between the dry strip you didn't wax and the wet wax will quickly disappear. Your floor will look better over a longer period of time, and your total maintenance time will be reduced significantly.

Frequency of rewaxing depends on the traffic in your home, the type and color of the floor, and the sort of abuse it is put through. Try to wax less often than you think is necessary. But your floor really tells you when it's time. It will start to look dull, and washing it doesn't really help. Generally speaking, after you've washed the floor regularly for three to six months (or washed it six to eight times), it will start to look as if it needs a new coat of wax. Kitchens will need another coat more often than laundry rooms, entryways more often than family rooms, and so forth. And all of these rooms more often than the bathroom because you're never going to wax in there.

Maintenance

You know that if no one ever walked on a floor, it would never need to be rewaxed. Armed with this bit of profundity, it's easy to understand that to reduce overall maintenance of the floor, you must reduce the damage done to the floor finish by foot traffic.

It's more important to sweep or vacuum the floor regularly that it is to wash it—even if it's the kitchen floor. Dirt particles on the floor are driven into the finish (or into the floor itself), which means the beginning of the end for the wax. Or dirt particles are ground between the floor finish and the soles of shoes, which has about the same general effect as using a mild sandpaper on the floor. The resulting little scratches cumulatively ruin the finish. Also, pick up or clean up anything that is spilled or dropped as soon as you can—not sometime in the future.

Sweeping or vacuuming daily would be ideal, especially if kids, pets, and heavy use prevail in your house. But even with less intense use, do so every few days. In Chapter 10, "Cleaning Carpets," we try to convince you to leave the vacuum out to make it more easily available for use. Running the vacuum over the major traffic areas of the carpets and floors every day should take less than 10 minutes in most homes. (Time yourself! It just seems longer.) Don't move the furniture or otherwise make it difficult for yourself. Just vacuum. Your floor finish will last much longer before it needs another coat of wax, and your floors will look better: no "dust bunnies" flying here and there, no pet hairs "everywhere." It's relaxing and so much more enjoyable to be in your home when you keep on top of the maintenance of it, instead of having that awful feeling that it's out of control. A few minutes a day. Try it.

Wash the kitchen floor with a very dilute solution of clear ammonia and water every couple of weeks. (We presume you don't have unsealed or waxed wood floors in the kitchen.) Do the family room once a month or so, and the entry once a week. This assumes that you're vacuuming the floors as advised. Needless to say, the less you vacuum, the more you must wash.

10   CLEANING CARPETS

You have a choice between several very different carpet-cleaning systems. As a quick review, and to make sure you have a chance to consider all the realistic options, here's a brief summary of all five major carpet-cleaning systems in current use. They include ones you can do yourself, as well as ones that professionals use. Needless to say, we have an opinion about them, and our recommendations follow.

Extraction

Widely and erroneously known as "steam cleaning," this is the method used by most professionals and is the method associated with most consumer rental equipment. It involves the injection of detergent and water (hot, warm, or cool—but definitely not steam) into the carpet under pressure, followed by the almost simultaneous wet-vacuuming (extraction) of the dirty solution. One variation of this method also involves agitation of the carpet with a brush located immediately after the hot-water nozzle and before the vacuum intake. *Advantages:* All things considered, this is the single method that cleans the deepest. The equipment is the easiest to find. *Disadvantages:* A significant amount of water can penetrate to the carpet backing and pad and remain there after extraction. If the carpet is badly soiled, this method requires agitation with a brush or rotary floor machine. Heavy units with a built-in brush can be awkward and backbreaking. The carpet requires a long time to dry. Hot water can set some stains permanently—for example, blood and sugar-based stains—so precleaning such stains is mandatory.

Rotary

This method uses a single-disc rotary floor machine. A rotary nylon brush directly scrubs cleaner into the carpet from a tank on the machine. The dirty solution is removed with a wet vacuum. *Advantages:* Cleans deeply by agitating the carpet fibers. If rotary and extraction methods are both used, the combination is the most effective approach for heavy soil. *Disadvantages:* Requires skill to avoid overwetting. Two machines are required: a floor machine and a wet vac. The carpet must be done in 4-foot by 4-foot areas or else the wet vac will not extract sufficient material. This method is almost always used in conjunction with the extractor method because of the inefficiency of the wet vac.

Foam

A machine applies cleaner in the form of foam that is scrubbed into the carpet with soft nylon reel brushes. The residue is removed with a wet vacuum. Some units have a wet vacuum built in, so the foam is removed almost immediately. Afterward, a thorough dry-vacuuming is recommended. *Advantages:* Foam prevents water from soaking deeply into the carpet. The carpet dries relatively quickly. *Disadvantages*: Not effective on heavy soiling. Residual cleaner can build up and cause resoiling. Spillage or overwetting can result in water damage. The equipment can be hard to find. The brushes can damage delicate fibers.

```
Dry Powder
```

This is a relatively new method in which dry absorbent material impregnated with dry-cleaning solvents and detergents is sprinkled onto the carpet and scrubbed into it with soft nylon reel or rotary brushes. The powder holds dirt in suspension and is dry-vacuumed away. *Advantages:* Absolutely no danger of water damage. Carpet can be walked on immediately. Powder can be used as an absorbent immediately after a spill. *Disadvantages:* Not effective on heavy soiling. The powder is difficult to vacuum out completely and can remain in the carpet and resoil it. The brushes used to work it into the carpet can damage delicate fibers.

```
Bonnet
```

A cotton or rayon absorbent pad (a "bonnet") is used with a single-disc rotary floor machine. Liquid carpet cleaner is applied with a sprayer or through the machine's tank in advance of the machine. *Advantages:* The carpet does not get deeply wet, so there is little risk of water damage, and it can be walked on almost immediately. There is relatively little danger of residual cleaner causing resoiling. *Disadvantages:* Not effective on heavy soil. The rotary motion can damage delicate fibers.

First, Deep-Clean the Carpet

Given this wide range of choices, what can be recommended for home use? Each method has its pros and cons. All require renting equipment and buying specialized supplies. The answer depends on how dirty the carpet is. If your carpet needs deep-down cleaning, we recommend that you hire a professional to get the job done right the first time. Ask what method the company proposes to use. We recommend that you do business with one that uses either of the two effective deep-cleaning methods: extraction or rotary followed by extraction.

If you want to deep-clean the carpet yourself, chances are that the available rental machine will be some form of an extraction device. Be careful not to soak the carpet and to dry it thoroughly afterward. You should recover 70 to 90% of the water going into the carpet. There is always a risk of damage: Moisture remaining in the carpet and/or its backing can seriously damage the carpet fibers, promote the growth of mildew, stretch and/or shrink the carpet, or damage the hardwood or subfloor underneath.

Maintenance Cleaning Using the Bonnet Method

Once the carpet is deep-cleaned (or if it's relatively new or already clean), here's a method of keeping it that way. Using this method, a carpet shouldn't have to be deep-cleaned again for months or years. That statement is absolute nonsense if you have a rugby team hanging out at your place, of course. (Every home has its own unique recleaning schedule!) But what we suggest is that you deep-clean the carpet only as needed—ideally only once—and that you institute an ongoing system of lighter-duty maintenance cleaning so your carpet will stay relatively clean all the time.

What's the best method for maintenance cleaning? It boils down to a choice between the bonnet and the dry-powder methods. If your carpets will tolerate absolutely no water, or if you cannot wait at all for the carpet to dry, then your only choice is the dry-powder method. But our first choice is the bonnet method. Its drying time is extremely brief—perhaps only 20 minutes, which is a good time to relax a bit. And you won't have to contend with residual powder in the carpet, as in the dry-powder method. Leftover solvent-laden powder continues to absorb dirt, and if you don't get it completely out of the carpet you'll begin to see respotting eventually.

The bonnet method cleans the top of the carpet—where most of the dirt will be accumulating anyway. The cleaner is lightly sprayed on top of the carpet, which makes it difficult to force dirt deeper into the carpet pile. It's then absorbed almost immediately by the absorbent bonnet, which is sort of a giant terry-cloth towel. You use a floor machine that works by spinning the bonnet on the carpet while the weight of the machine holds the bonnet flat against the carpet, where it can absorb the cleaner and dirt very efficiently. If you think about it, the method is really a reliable spot-cleaning method on a large scale. Instead of using a cleaning cloth and spotting solution, you are using a bonnet and liquid carpet cleaner. Safe, reliable, and effective.

Finding the Equipment

The bonnet method requires a floor machine and a supply of bonnets. The floor machine is the same type used to strip wax from resilient floors (see Chapter 8, "Stripping Floors"), so you might be able to get double your money's worth by renting it for both purposes over a marathon weekend. You should be able to find it at any full-service rental outlet. It's true that you will have to lug home a machine to do this job, but the equipment is no more bulky than a traditional extraction carpet machine.

Be sure the floor machine you rent is 17 inches or less in diameter. Larger than that is too big for home use. Insist that the salesperson give you a demonstration or good instructions on how to operate and control it. The machine is easy to handle only *after* you know how. Otherwise, it will seem too difficult and it can easily result in torn (or very tired) muscles and/or damage to your baseboards or furniture.

The bonnets are not expensive and can be washed and reused over and over, but they will be more difficult to locate than the floor machine. You can try a local janitorial supply house or order them from our catalog. They come in sizes corresponding to the diameter of the floor machine's disc, so first call the rental store and find out what size floor machine they have. Then order that size bonnet. Using a 17-inch machine, you'll need one or two bonnets for a 10-foot by 10-foot room with a moderately soiled carpet.

MATERIALS

   1 17-inch or smaller single-disc floor machine
1–2 bonnets per room (the same diameter as the floor-machine disc)
   1 bottle of carpet cleaner (most nonfoaming carpet cleaners, especially Red Juice, will work well)
   1 pump-up pressure sprayer (or spray bottle)
   1 measuring cup
   1 cleaning apron
   5 cleaning cloths
   1 spray bottle of Red Juice
   1 toothbrush
   1 vacuum cleaner (the "Big Vac")

Preparation

Remove all the furniture that you must. One of the rationalizations we think you use to put off cleaning the carpet so long is that you don't want to move all that furniture. So don't. Move only those pieces that can get dirt under them. Like the coffee table, but not the couch. Like the dining-room table and chairs, but not the TV. Like the end tables, but not the china cabinet. See how much easier this is getting?

While dirt can't get under the couch too easily, it can—and does—accumulate right up to the edge of it. So slide the couch back two inches. That way you can get the last bit of dirt that was there, but you avoid lifting it. Some pieces of furniture don't even need to be moved at all—like a console television. Usually you don't need to move the bed—but if you do, just move it a few inches one way and then a few more back the other way. Put aluminum foil or plastic wrap under the legs of any furniture on damp areas of the carpet.

You know by now not to try to move any of these heavy things by yourself. You also don't want to drag heavy furniture across the carpet unless you are fond of ripples in the carpet, which will cause more grief than the entire carpet-cleaning process.

But do move everything out of the way that you are going to ultimately have to move. Now, before you start cleaning. Include the little things like the magazine holder, potted plants, the stack of newspapers, and so forth. Clear the decks.

Thoroughly vacuum all the carpeting you are going to clean. Use a vacuum with a reel-type brush and beater bar to do a deep cleaning.

Mixing the Carpet Cleaner

Mix the carpet-cleaning solution directly in the pump-up pressure sprayer. As usual, follow the manufacturer's directions. Wear your cleaning apron so you can carry the sprayer in a pocket or on an apron loop when not in use. Your apron is also handy for carrying a few cleaning cloths for any spills, as well as a toothbrush if you need to give some extra attention to a spot.

Traffic Areas, Spots, and Stains

You must make two trips around the room for two different jobs. The *first* trip is to pretreat any spots or stains by lightly spraying them first with the carpet-cleaning solution. Also pretreat the dirtier traffic areas: for example, the entrance areas, the area in front of the couch, or the paths from the kitchen to just about everywhere else.

Use your toothbrush to agitate any spots or stains that look like they may not come up easily. If there are a whole bunch of little horrors, you may want to treat them with the methods described in Chapter 11, "Spot-Cleaning Carpets," before you start cleaning the entire carpet.

Applying Carpet Cleaner

On the *second* trip, lightly spray the whole carpet to be cleaned. This includes respraying the traffic areas and spots you had already pretreated.

Spray and clean one room at a time. Start in the left corner farthest from the exit door. Spray the cleaner evenly and thoroughly in 3-foot strips, moving all the way from one side of the room to the other with each strip. Hold the sprayer nozzle 2 feet or so from the surface. Don't spray under furniture if the floor machine won't fit there *unless* you want to hand-clean those areas. If so, you can use a cleaning cloth to absorb the cleaner and dirt. Don't spray areas that aren't dirty. Examples are corners or other areas where there is little or no traffic.

It's a little difficult to be sure that you've completely sprayed an area. To help keep track, pick or create a landmark in the room each time you make a new pass. For example, spot where you are in relation to the TV or another piece of furniture each time you start a new 3-foot strip. Or put down a cleaning cloth to mark your spot. When you've covered the entire carpet, you're ready to use the floor machine.

If the carpet is only lightly soiled, you can start scrubbing with the bonnet immediately after applying the cleaner. For moderately soiled carpet, wait 5 minutes. If heavily soiled, wait 10.

Steering It

The secret to using a floor machine is to control its movement and direction by very slightly raising or lowering the handle. These *subtle* changes cause the rotating brush to have a little more traction on the front or back of the brush, which in turn causes the machine to move to the right or to the left. Your first (often somewhat hysterical) impulse is to try to change direction of the machine by brute force, which even a very strong person can barely do. Using muscle power alone won't stop the machine in time if it wants to go somewhere (for example, through the glass coffee table). If the machine all of a sudden seems to have a mind of its own and is heading straight for mayhem, let go of the handle. The machine will stop because it's equipped with a safety trigger. Thank goodness. Reminds me of a wonderful story about learning to water-ski and forgetting to let go of the rope after falling, but that's another subject.

Once you try (and remember) the simple up-and-down steering tactic, the machine is easy enough to operate. It doesn't require particular strength, just attention, so just about anyone should be able to tackle this job.

For the sake of your back, find a comfortable level at which to hold the floor-machine handle (usually just below the waist). If you hold it too high, someone may have to massage your shoulders afterward. If you hold it too low, your lower back will let you know promptly.

The best way to manage the long power cord and to keep it out of your way is to put it over one shoulder while the machine is in operation. Also, run the cord out the exit door and into an electrical outlet that isn't in the room in which you're working. Wear an old shirt or blouse because the cord is apt to be dirty. And wear nonslip tennis shoes for traction.

The Starting Point

Move the floor machine to the corner of the room where you started spraying the carpet cleaner. To install a bonnet, tilt the machine back and center the bonnet on the rotary brush. Press the bonnet into place and restore the machine to its normal upright position. The bonnet is held in place by the weight of the machine on top of it. Keep a supply of spare bonnets close by. Until you know more about how this process works on your carpets, be sure to check the bonnet frequently to see how soiled it has become. You can check less often once you know how long each side of the bonnet lasts. Turn it over as soon as it's too dirty to absorb more solution. Replace it with a new one when both sides are soiled. Of course, once the bonnet is saturated with dirt and cleaning solution it loses its ability to clean any further.

The Strategy

The strategy is simple enough. Work your way to the right across the room. Then back up a little less than the diameter of the floor machine, and start working back to the left—overlapping the original pass slightly. If you've sprayed areas the machine will not reach, do them by hand using a cleaning cloth. (Stop the machine to do these areas as you come to them.) Rub the cleaning cloth back and forth a few times over the sprayed carpet to absorb the dirt and cleaning solution.

Reach for your toothbrush and Red Juice if there are small spots that need working. Be careful not to damage the carpet fiber with the toothbrush. A gentle agitation is all that's needed. The Red Juice will help on most spots that are still holding out. Blot it up afterward with another cleaning cloth.

As you progress, try to manage the cord so you don't run over it with the floor machine. It doesn't appreciate it any more than you would.

When you finish cleaning the carpet, pop the bonnets into the washing machine and set it to "stun." Load the floor machine back into the car and return it to the rental store while the carpet dries . . . unless you have a saintly rental store that picks up and delivers. If you're ambitious and have taken your vitamins for the day, you might want to use the same floor machine to strip the wax from the kitchen floor. Or you may just want to put your feet up and admire your sparkling clean carpet.

The Finishing Touch

When the carpet is completely dry, vacuum it thoroughly once more. It should take as little as 20 minutes to dry using the bonnet method. But if you're in a cold climate, or if you applied too much cleaner, or if you need to hasten drying time, here's how.

Drying Out the Carpet

After any carpet-cleaning method that uses water, if the carpet feels wet to the touch you may want to speed the drying process—either to make it usable more quickly or to minimize the possibility of mildew. One very effective way of drying out the carpet relies on the fact that warm air can carry much more moisture than cold air. Heat the room thoroughly to bring the water out of the carpet and into the room air. Then open all the windows and doors and replace the moist warm air with dry cool air. Close the room up again and repeat this cycle a few times until the carpet feels dry to the touch and there is no wet or soapy smell in the room. You'll be amazed how quickly this procedure will dry out the carpet. A rotating room fan can also help speed the process along.

As soon as the carpet is dry and the vacuuming is finished, you can move the furniture back in and start using the room again. If you maintain your carpet with this method as often as needed (maybe once or twice a year), you will always have a great-looking carpet and will rarely have to do a deep extraction cleaning. Besides, you will get so good at using the floor machine that the whole process will get easier and easier. Congratulations.

Maintenance and Prevention Between Cleanings

Step 1

The single most important thing you can do to keep your carpet clean is to vacuum it regularly. It seems to us that one reason people resist such a straightforward task as vacuuming is because it's too much trouble to "drag the vacuum out" of wherever it's kept between uses. If that's your excuse, store the vacuum somewhere else. You could even leave it out most of the time—in a corner or somewhere out of the way. Maybe then you would use it daily (if you have kids and pets, for example) or every few days (if not). Stuff it back into the closet when company comes—but only if you promise to bring it back out when they leave.

The other excuse we hear is that the vacuum is too heavy. If that is the case, please replace it as quickly as you can afford to with one that you can manage. A lot of the older uprights actually aren't too heavy. It's just that their suction makes them grab onto the surface in a way that can make them awkward to move. Now there are even rechargeable, cordless electric vacuums that are very light and easy to use. And *fast!* Maybe you could check into purchasing one of these even before you replace the vacuum that you don't use. (It takes soooooooo very long to wear out something you never use.) Lightweight portables may still have to be supplemented by a deeper-cleaning standard vacuum, but if you're not vacuuming at all they're certainly better than what you're doing now.

Step 2

The second maintenance step is to clean up spills (you know, those things that turn into spots and stains) as they occur. Very few spills are all that horrendous if you take care of them *immediately*. Red Juice is an extraordinarily broad-based cleaner and will do an excellent job on a wide range of carpet offenses. Keep a bottle handy, together with a toothbrush and cleaning cloths or a roll of paper towels. See Chapter 11, "Spot-Cleaning Carpets," especially the section on how to remove those accidents before they become stains.

Step 3

Use mats, runners, or throw rugs to protect the house in general and your carpets in particular. Most of the dirt that ends up in your house came in through the doors—up to 85% of it, according to some authorities. You can reduce your housecleaning burden tremendously by using mats to catch most of that dirt in its concentrated form before it is disbursed throughout the house.

The correct placement of the mats is both inside and outside the exterior doors of your home. The larger the mat the better: More dirt will be wiped off. Ideally, each mat would cover four or five steps on both sides of the door, although this is bigger than most of us have room for. We recommend that the mat outside the door be the typical rubber-backed mat that you are used to seeing in store entrances. But don't use a rubber-backed mat inside the house on a vinyl or asphalt floor because it may discolor the floor.

Don't forget that the other thing you want the mat to catch (besides dirt) is water. Get a mat or carpet of a material that will absorb the water, not repel it. Inside the house, we prefer a carpet mat that can be thrown in the washing machine.

Don't let the mats themselves get saturated with dirt or they won't do any good at all—rather like trying to catch dripping water in a pot that is overflowing with each new drop. Maintain the mats by shaking or vacuuming them daily (or nearly so). It makes sense to have two sets, so you can put out a clean, dry set when one set gets wet or is being washed. Also, now that you're going to have such nice clean carpets using the bonnet cleaning method, use a nice-looking throw rug on an area of carpet that is worn—even if it isn't at a door. This improves the appearance of the whole room and enhances the overall result of your other cleaning efforts.

One note of caution. Occasionally we see homes with a patch of carpet remnant used as a mat directly on the carpet beneath without an intervening rubber or jute pad. As it comes from the same roll of carpet, it may seem to be a reasonable practice. Unfortunately, the backing of carpeting is much more abrasive than the fibers themselves. If the backing is placed directly on the surface of a carpet without a protective pad, every footstep will wear away a bit of the lower carpet as though it were being sandpapered. A protective pad is mandatory and very inexpensive. And nobody should have to tell you to put a nonslip pad under a throw rug if it's used on a hardwood or other slippery floor.

As with most maintenance, these ideas will cost some money to implement, and they take a little time to perform on a regular basis. The payoff is that they reduce the overall time you spend cleaning the house—so you might actually have some leisure time left over on weekends for a change. And you'll have a nicer home to live in and enjoy that will avoid the violent swings between *very clean* and *very dirty* that are so frustrating and, ultimately, time-consuming.

11 SPOT-CLEANING CARPETS

Spots in fabrics are outside the scope of this book, but you'll certainly be running into a few carpet spots or stains as you make your way through spring cleaning. "Stain" and "spot" are often used interchangeably, but a consensus exists that a stain is the more permanent of the two. "Stain" is the term your dry cleaner will use, for example, when you bring in what you thought was an innocent little spot: "*This?* You want me to clean *this?* Oh, no, that's a *stain.*"

We will be optimistic and refer to most messes on the carpet as spots. If they remain despite your best efforts, at least you'll know exactly what to call them. First we'll discuss how to treat spots. Then we'll move on to stains.

Treating Spots

Needless to say, one of the best ways to prevent a spot from evolving into a stain is to act on the spot immediately, before it has time to go though whatever unwelcome chemical transformations it has in mind. The first thing to do is to blot up as much of the material as possible with a supply of clean, dry cloths. Next apply a modest amount of cool water and blot up the spill with cleaning cloths. If the spot might also stain your cleaning cloths, you might prefer to use paper towels. White Bounty Microwave towels are the best we've found to date.

Work from the edge inward, turning the cloth often. Don't rub back and forth, or you may drive the spill into the fiber. Instead, *twist* the cloth as you blot. This twisting motion will work the material to the surface more effectively than rubbing back and forth.

Next, spray the area with Red Juice, agitate with the toothbrush if needed, and blot up. After you've blotted up all the moisture you can, place several dry cloths or paper towels over the area. Weight them down with books for a few hours to keep pressure on the area and to help absorb remaining moisture and soil. Red Juice turns out to be one of the best all-around spot removers that we've ever seen—in many cases working when specialty spotting products have failed. We've seen it lift coffee spots right out of carpets after the spots had been neglected for weeks! It can work miracles on all carpet fibers except those whose dyes are not colorfast (which are rare these days). You might want to test an area now so you'll be able to act immediately if an emergency arises.

If you have a wet-dry vacuum, that is the remedy recommended by the bible of the carpet industry, *The How-to Handbook of Carpets*. This use, plus its back-saving contribution to floor cleaning, makes a wet-dry vac pay for itself many times over. If you have one, start by wet-vacuuming the spot. Next, apply cool water with a cleaning cloth or sponge and revacuum. Continue these two steps, and you may find the spot completely gone. You can also treat the spot with Red Juice, agitate with the toothbrush, flush with water, and then wet-vac again. Finish by placing several dry cloths or paper towels weighted down over the area, as in the manual method.

If you can't interrupt what you're doing to treat a spot sufficiently—let's say you're in the middle of a dinner for the ambassador—many carpet-cleaning professionals recommend that you sprinkle an absorbent powder on the spot when it's still wet. Traditional absorbents are cornstarch, corn meal, talcum powder, and carpet dry-cleaning powder (e.g., Host). Trouble is, the absorbent can be a problem getting out of the carpet, too, especially if you have a dark rug. If you have the dry-cleaning powder, that's the absorbent of first choice.

One of the most frequent spills on carpets is red wine. You will often hear that the best antidote is to douse the spot with white wine. It does appear to work, through a chemical reaction, but you risk saturating the carpet backing with the resulting concoction and doing far more serious damage. You're better off using conventional spot-treatment techniques.

By necessity, we're going to offer two tactics for treating spots that have had a chance to set: *fast* and *fussy*. Naturally, we recommend that you try the fast approach first. Failing that, you'll have to resort to a particular treatment for that type of stain.

```
┌─────────────────┐
│      FAST       │
└─────────────────┘
```

MATERIALS

    1 spray bottle of Red Juice
    1 spray bottle of plain water
    1 toothbrush
    1 scraper
 5–10 cotton cleaning cloths or a roll of paper towels
    1 carryall tray

Preparation

With any luck at all, the majority of stains afflicting your carpet can be banished with Red Juice, the toothbrush, and cotton cloths. Red Juice is a cleaner with a deliberately wide range of effectiveness, and its formula is not dangerous to any type of fiber that we've yet to discover after several years of field experience. Having said that, it is still prudent to check *any* cleaner on an inconspicuous area of the carpet. We know it's aggravating to read that warning over and over (sort of like those annoying tags on furniture that say never to remove them). Unfortunately there is little other choice unless you are fond of gambling. You should only have to do this test once . . . per carpet . . . per cleaner. Sorry.

The carpet should be vacuumed before attempting to treat a spot. It's rare to be able to solve the problem with vacuuming alone, but removing as much of the material as possible will help your efforts along. Who knows, you may be lucky enough to find that the "stain" is really just a deposit of fine powder.

Treating the Stain

Approach the stain. Do not be afraid. You are bigger than it is. (We hope.) Treatment is best done on hands and knees to spare your back. If your knees need sparing, too, and if you have a hoard of spots on the rug, you might consider knee pads. They look odd but your knees won't care.

Okay, okay, this is *one* case where the cleaning apron can be less effective than the carryall tray. You'll be on your hands and knees, and it can be difficult to remove and replace the cleaning tools in and out of the apron without stopping to straighten up. Best to keep them in the tray in between uses along with the Red Juice, cleaning cloths, and other supplies. If you're cleaning many spots in close proximity, just keep pushing the tray in front of you on the carpet as you make your way along.

The fast approach to a generic spot is to spray it full blast with Red Juice, agitate reasonably gently with the toothbrush, and then blot up with the cleaning cloths or paper towels. Don't be bashful with the Red Juice. In fact, it's best to set the nozzle more toward "stun" than to the fine setting. On the other hand, don't soak through to the carpet backing. If the stain turns out to be a solid mass of something unfortunate, you may have to break it up with the scraper before proceeding any further with the toothbrush.

Remember that blotting has a little trick to it. Just as when you are treating an immediate spill, you don't want to rub the stain back into the carpet after you've dislodged the dirt with Red Juice and the toothbrush. So *twist* the cloth as you blot. Again, turn the cloth over and replace it with a clean one as often as needed so you are always blotting with a clean and dry area of the cloth. As the cleaning cloths become too wet or dirty to use, throw them into the cleaning tray. It's all in the wrist.

Carpet treatment requires one extra step as a precaution against restaining. If even a modest amount of cleaning agent remains in the carpet, it can hold on to new dirt more so than adjoining areas. Hence the puzzling phenomenon of treated areas getting *worse* after they're treated.

To head this regrettable event off at the pass, you need to flush *any* cleaner from the carpet after you've finished blotting. The safest means is plain water applied with a spray bottle followed by more blotting. Don't soak the carpet; just use enough water to flush out any remaining cleaning agent.

Small damp areas (a few inches) can be blotted dry. Larger areas should be covered with dry cleaning cloths and weighted down with books for a few hours to remove additional moisture and soil from the carpet.

The proper finishing touch is to brush the nap of the carpet in the area you just cleaned and neutralized. When they dry, fibers will adopt the shape and direction in which you left them wet, so why ask for trouble? Just take a moment to reset the nap by brushing lightly against the grain of the carpet. When it dries, you shouldn't be able to notice the difference between the area you treated and the surrounding areas. And it won't restain either. If you have a long shag rug, you can buy a specialized nap brush to reset the nap. Ask at a janitorial specialty store.

FUSSY

By now it's definitely time to call them stains instead of spots, presuming that they have remained in place long enough to pose a serious threat to removal. The number of potential carpet stains is limitless. And if you review the literature, you'll find a bewildering number of different (and often contradictory) recommendations. To simplify matters to a reasonable degree, we have gathered stains into three major categories. Once you understand what type of stain you're dealing with, the treatments are reasonably uniform per type. One thing all these treatments have in common is that they require pretesting.

Type 1: Solvent Stains

All the stains in this category are dissolved by dry-cleaning–type solvents and *not* by water. They are what would be commonly called oily or greasy stains. They usually appear as dark stains on the carpet, and they usually trap dirt more and more over time.

Examples include:

airplane glue	furniture polish	rubber cement
asphalt	glue, household	shoe polish
ballpoint-pen ink	grease	tar
butter	lacquer	varnish
cosmetics	oil	wax
fat	petroleum jelly	

Treatment

Removing these stains requires a solvent. Technically, water is a solvent—it dissolves things like sugar—but when most people use the term they are referring to the more common understanding of a solvent as a heavy-duty agent. In particular, there are two classifications of solvent that merit our attention (based on Professor Herb Brandt's terminology):

OIL-BASED SOLVENTS	COMBINATION SOLVENTS

Carbona
Lacquer thinner
Lighter fluid
Professional
   dry-cleaning
   fluid
	Magic
	Shout
	Spray 'n Wash

Oil-based solvents dissolve a stain, mix with it, and then evaporate—leaving a powdery residue behind or none at all. They are potentially very powerful agents, so they must be used with due respect and after the usual pretesting in that same inconspicuous spot we keep talking about. Depending on the makeup of your carpet, some solvents can be harmful to the fabric or to the backing, so several other precautions apply: (1) Do not use on a wet stain. Oil-based solvents and water don't get along. (2) Make sure the room is well ventilated. The fumes don't get along with your liver. (3) Don't saturate the carpet with the solvent. You don't want to soak the backing of the carpet with it. (4) Always wear gloves when working with oil-based solvents.

Among the oil-based solvents listed, our strong preference is for lacquer thinner—a mxiture of acetone and several other strong solvents. It's relatively cheap and can be amazingly effective on grease, oil, wax, and gum. It dissolves without leaving a residue. Actually, it is one of the most powerful cleaning agents commonly available—provided it doesn't dissolve the surface you're cleaning. It is safe for most carpet fibers (test first, of course), but it will dissolve many plastics and painted surfaces. Don't pour it into a Styrofoam cup while you're working with it because it will eat right through the bottom. It will also dissolve the plastic bristles of some brushes.

Lighter fluid is another superb oil-based solvent that has many applications. It is far less destructive to a surface than is lacquer thinner, but it will leave an oil stain on porous surfaces like flat-finished walls or wallpaper, and it is therefore ill advised for those applications. It is an absolute pleasure to use on the residue of gummy labels (e.g., price tags) and adhesive tape. Readers who have been cleaning for a few years will recall that kerosene used to be one of the main household cleaners. Its effectiveness is very similar to lighter fluid.

Carbona is a quality retail dry-cleaning fluid that has many of the cleaning abilities of lacquer thinner but again is less destructive to many surfaces. If you are on friendly terms with your local dry cleaner, you might persuade him or her to sell you a small supply of professional dry-cleaning fluid.

Here come the warnings: These and other oil-based solvents are highly flammable.

Do not use them near an open flame (e.g., a pilot light of an appliance like a water heater). Store them prudently between uses. Do not use them on an antique or fine Oriental rug because its dyes may not stand up to the treatment.

Combination solvents are a recent development that mix a solvent and glycerin, soap, and/or water. They evaporate so slowly that it's only theoretical, so they must be rinsed after the stain is treated—which requires an extra step or two and extra time. They are more conservative treatments than the oil solvents, but they do not generate obnoxious fumes.

To treat stains with a combination solvent, the safest way to proceed is to apply the solvent to a cleaning cloth—not the carpet itself. Just place it over the stain and apply pressure without rubbing. Check the cloth. If some of the material is transferring to the cloth, you're in business. Blot toward the middle of the stain, rotating to new and clean areas of the cloth wet with the solvent. When the stain appears to be gone, place a stack of five to six dry cleaning cloths over the stain and put a weight on top to absorb the solvent. Remove the cloths after a few hours. This is a fine use for your otherwise worn-out cleaning cloths. If you are using your regular cleaning cloths, make sure you launder them before using them for other cleaning tasks.

The above procedure is deliberately cautious. If the stain does not respond, you may want to up the ante by agitating the stain with the toothbrush. Use reasonable caution, and work toward the center of the stain so you don't spread it. After you've loosened the stain with the brush, blot up with clean cloths. After you get to know how much your carpet will tolerate, you may be able to shift to using the toothbrush right away. As always when using the toothbrush on a carpet, reset the nap by brushing lightly after treating the spot.

If you've used an oil-based solvent and a powdery residue remains, it should come right up with a vacuum cleaner. If you've used a combination solvent, you've got to remove the solvent/stain mixture after treatment. Blot it up as best you can with clean cloths, and follow with a Red Juice treatment and blot. Finally, flush and then blot with cool water.

Type 2: Water-Based Stains

All the stains in this category are dissolved by water or a water-based solution. Alas, there are many subcategories. Although oil-based solvents are powerful agents, they are of little or no use on stains in this category.

Digestive Stains

Removal of these stains requires that they be broken down with digestive enzymes. Examples include:

animal glue	cream	gravy
blood	eggs	ice cream
body fluids	feces	milk
bugs, squished	gelatin	vomit

You can choose from a variety of digestive enzymes:

amylase	**papain**
Axion	**pepsin**
Biz	**spit**

Bet I know which one caught your attention. Yes, good old spit (saliva if you are a formal person) is a collection of some dandy digestive enzymes. More than one restorer has taken a priceless oil painting into the workshop and dabbed at a noble visage with a cotton swab moistened with . . . spit! Works wonders. Look how well it cleans eyeglasses. But your carpet stain probably needs more than dabbing with a cotton swab, so you're more likely to use Axion or Biz. The other enzymes can be even more effective, but they require a trip to a good drugstore.

Enzymes are applied as a paste. If you have a wet-dry vac, first flush the area with warm water and extract it with the vacuum. If not, apply a little warm water to help speed the enzymes along. But don't soak the carpet. Wear rubber gloves, as you wouldn't want the paste to start digesting your hands along with the stain. (Just kidding . . . sort of.) Mix equal parts of water and enzyme to make a paste. Work it into the stain with your gloved fingers. Leave the paste in place for half an hour. If it dries out before then, add a little bit of warm water. It's best to keep the area warm to promote activity by the enzymes. If possible, apply hot towels over the mixture for up to 20 minutes.

To remove the paste, flush with warm water. Extract the water with the wet vac if you have one. If not, blot it up with a healthy supply of clean cloths. Reset the nap with the toothbrush. If the area still feels damp, place a weighted pile of four to six dry cloths on top of the area.

Tannin Stains

These are usually tan or brown in color, odorless, and difficult to remove. They include:

alcoholic beverages	grass	tea
beer	inks—certain types	tobacco
coffee	leaves	wine
fruit juice	soft drinks	

Tannin stains are difficult to treat. You'll need to make a potion. Wear gloves while preparing it. The formula recommended by *The How-to Handbook of Carpets* is as follows:

> 1 oz. (2 tablespoons) oxalic acid
> ½ oz. (1 T) glacial acetic acid or white vinegar
> 4 oz. (8 T) glycerin
> butyl (not rubbing) alcohol

Mix the oxalic acid and glacial acetic acid or white vinegar. Add the glycerin and stir. Continue stirring while adding enough butyl (not rubbing) alcohol to make the mixture clear. Oxalic acid (it's toxic, so be careful with it!) can be found at a hardware store in the paint section, as it is widely used as a rust remover. It might be labeled "wood bleach." The other ingredients may require a trip to the drugstore unless someone in the house is a chemist. Glycerin—a mild solvent—is used to soften the stain.

Apply this potion and leave it in place *for a few minutes only*. Wear gloves, of course, and blot up the potion/stain mess with the clean cloths. Flush with water and reblot or extract with the wet vac. The cleaning cloths are ready for the laundry.

Metallic Stains

Caused by the deposit or one or more metals, these stains appear as a powdrey smear. The color is the clue to what type of stain it is: a green stain is from copper or brass, while a brown stain is from iron rust.

Treatment of the stain will depend on the type of metal. Iron-rust stains call for oxalic acid. Start with a solution of 2 tablespoons per cup of warm water. If your carpet can stand it, you may have to increase the concentration. Apply the solution with a toothbrush.

Copper and brass stains call for white vinegar. Use it full strength. For any kind of metal stains, of course, you will have pretested an area. Follow by treatment with Red Juice or a spotting solution and the usual blotting or extraction techniques.

Dye or Pigment Stains

Stains caused by agents that were intended to stain in the first place are formidable adversaries. Other substances, such as medicines, have similar effects. Examples include:

colored paper	medicines
furniture dyes	watercolors
iodine (call a professional)	wet inks

Try full-strength white vinegar followed by Red Juice or a spotter. If the spot remains, try a solution of 1 part clear ammonia to 4 parts water. Agitate, blot, or extract as usual. Don't get your hopes up. You'll probably be making a call to a professional.

Emulsifiable Wet Stains

These are stiff, crusty stains that will usually respond to detergent cleaners. Components of the stain can be emulsified or suspended in the cleaning agent.

This is the "if all else fails, call it this" category. These stains should respond to Red Juice or to a specialty rug-spotting detergent product. Remove all dry material with a vacuum or your scraper first. Then spray with Red Juice, agitate with the toothbrush, and blot up. Follow with a water flush and final blotting.

Type 3: Combination Stains

This type of stain is a mixture of both the solvent and water-based stains. For example, coffee with cream and sugar has both types of stains. First treat it as a solvent stain and then as a water-based stain.

Chewing Gum

What discussion of carpet stains would be complete without mention of Carpet Public Enemy No. 1—chewing gum? Most of us have heard of the standard solution: Rub the offending wad with ice and then it's supposed to pop right off. Trouble is, that hardly ever works. It takes forever and your fingers turn blue. Professionals use a blast of freon or carbon dioxide—eminently colder and faster, but potentially hazardous in the hands of the untrained.

According to our local carpet-cleaning authority, Frank Gromm, the freezing method only really works when the wad of gum is resting on the surface of the carpet. Once it gets smushed into the carpet fibers, freezing it isn't going to do much good at all. If you do want to try, *The How-to Handbook of Carpets* recommends that you protect the carpet by cutting a hole in a piece of cardboard the size of the gum. Use the cardboard as a shield to prevent freezing the carpet or scattering pieces of frozen gum. Rub the gum with ice until it freezes, and then whack it smartly with the back of a tablespoon to dislodge the gum. Finish off any remaining gum with an oil-based solvent like lacquer thinner and follow with a Red Juice treatment.

In most cases, the gum is pressed into the carpet too deeply to bother with ice. Try lacquer thinner patiently. It will dissolve the gum, but you'll have to work at it awhile. Wet an old cleaning cloth or piece of terry-cloth towel with lacquer thinner and work at the gum toward the center of the blotch. Follow with a Red Juice treatment.

Cigarette Burns

If the burn is severe enough, of course, a professional has to be called in to repair the carpet. Minor burns can be treated by vacuuming first with the long nozzle to generate high suction. Then lightly sand the edges of the burn with coarse sandpaper and vacuum again. If necessary, follow with a treatment of Red Juice or spotter solution plus blotting.

Miscellaneous Do-Nots

- Do not use rubbing alcohol to treat stains. It contains water and other ingredients and may cause problems. Go to the drugstore for butyl alcohol if alcohol is called for.

- Do not use lacquer thinner or acetone on acetate or triacetate carpets. They will turn to froth right in front of you.

- Do not apply heat to a fruit, blood, or sugar stain. In general, if you don't know what a stain is, don't apply heat.

- Do not use acids on blood. They may set the stain permanently.

Passing the Buck

As complex as the above may sound, we really just barely scratched the surface of the subject. Red Juice is such a good cleaner that you probably won't have to invoke one of the more labor-intensive treatments just reviewed. If you had to, and if it didn't work, you have a choice about your next step.

Plan A

Consult the literature for more detailed information about your particular stain. There are several excellent sources:

Brandt, Herb. *How to Remove Spots and Stains.* (New York: Putnam, 1987.) A lucid, scholarly, and eminently helpful book. Covers amazing stains like hoisin sauce and coleslaw. The best book on the subject to date.

Moore, Alma Chestnut. *How to Clean Everything.* (New York: Simon & Schuster, 1952.) A classic in the field with many subsequent editions.

The U.S. Government Publications Office has a variety of publications on treatments of stains.

Plan B

Call in a professional. Professionals have access to the latest chemical advances in specific stain treatments, which are being made with encouraging frequency these days. You should call in a professional early in your response to a stain if you have a delicate, valuable, or antique rug.

12 POLISHING METALS

Cleaning metallic surfaces throughout the house is inevitably an aspect of routine weekly cleaning. Aluminum shower frames, appliances, lamps, and so forth all have metal surfaces that can be treated with standard cleaning methods. But this chapter is concerned with the polishing or special care of metals that is not part of routine cleaning. Such treatment also requires metal polishes and cloths that you normally don't carry with you during your routine cleaning rounds.

Silver

Primary among the metals that would require an occasional special cleaning is silver. Properly polished silver has a deep luster that is worth the effort to attain it. But it is a relatively soft metal, which is enough to convince us to begin our discussion of cleaning methods with a few warnings about how to avoid scratching it or otherwise damaging it. It's far better to be too cautious with silver than too experimental, as many effects cannot be reversed.

Do-Nots

The first "do not" warning is not to use any of the quick electrolytic methods you may have heard about—you know, submerging the silver in a chemical potion in the kitchen sink with aluminum foil at the bottom. The method works almost instantaneously, but it does its job too well. It can strip the surface of the deep patina that develops over time on silver and can leave it dull and porous-looking. It can also strip the oxidation deliberately applied by the silversmith—darker areas that emphasize detail and create depth.

Likewise, many authorities frown on another fast method: silver dip. Although highly reputable companies sell the product, it is considered to be too harsh on the silver's oxidation and may leave an unnatural finish.

Silver experts are united in their opinion that heavy rubbing must be avoided to prevent scratches. A high-quality polish will do its work without bearing down on the surface. Relax and let the polish do its duty. Similarly, machine-buffing—even by a jeweler—is frowned upon. And nobody has to tell you not to use heavy abrasive powders on silver. Every silver polish that we have seen has abrasive powder as one of its ingredients, but it is an exceedingly fine powder almost like talcum. The same idea, but a far cry from Comet, Ajax, or even Bon Ami.

Choice of Polish

If you visit a good hardware store you'll be confronted with a dazzling array of polishes. The first decision is between polishes specialized for silver versus those suitable for many metals.

Specialized polishes split into ones that are rinsed off under water and ones that are wiped off. Goddard's makes a particularly distinguished line of silver polishes, several of which are recommended by various authorities.

Those who have pitched their tent in the camp of the generalized metal polishes prefer to have fewer specialized cleaning products cluttering up the house. Provided that the polish does not do too harsh a job on the silver surface, generalized cleaners can do excellent work. The one that comes recommended most often is Flintoline, a product made in Holland and consisting of turpentine, ammonia, and French rouge (an exceedingly mild abrasive).

You may have noticed that we're being somewhat noncommittal on this subject. Personal choice and traditions are large factors here. Also, silver can vary so widely in composition, age, and use that it is difficult to make an absolute recommendation. Rather, we will spend most of our efforts discussing methods of polishing silver rather than picking out the polish itself.

So Fast It's Almost Cheating

If the silver is not heavily tarnished, you may be able to get away with a cute trick. Just spray the piece with Red Juice and wipe off with a cleaning cloth! Many liquid cleaners can work minor miracles. We *did* say minor. It won't make much difference if it's been neglected for a year or so, and it won't impress the Queen. But you will remove a thin layer of surface tarnish—enough to let you squeak by unless Betty and Phil are stopping by.

The Real Thing

Okay, it's time to bring out the polish and have at it. Put on some old clothes that you won't mind getting splattered with polish. Clear off an ample work surface and cover it with something to protect it, if needed. Newspaper is not the best choice because the newsprint can transfer to the silver. Old towels or rags would do nicely and would soften the damage if you were to drop a large piece on the table. First make sure the silver is not covered with any sort of grit that could be ground into the surface by polishing. If needed, give the silver a preliminary bath under running water or with Red Juice sprayed freely.

Regardless of the polish you have selected, our general approach is the same. Apply the polish sparingly with a soft cotton cloth. Small pieces of an old terry-cloth towel are terrific. If you're using a liquid polish, it's faster to pour a little polish into a shallow dish so you don't have to pick up the bottle over and over. If the silver is only moderately tarnished, just rub gently with the cloth.

If the tarnish is heavy or if the surface is irregular, rub gently with a real toothbrush. The bristles of our heavy-duty brush are too thick and stiff to be useful here. Make sure the toothbrush you use is rated *soft*. Alternatively, both Goddard and Hagerty both sell a specialized silver brush made of hair.

By now you've made a fine mess of polish and tarnish. Don't wait until it dries to a powder. Wipe it from the surface with another soft cloth. If it's a flat surface, that's all you may have to do. If it's irregular, another step is needed. Spray the surface with Red or Blue Juice to rid it of residual polish that is about to dry into a visible powder that will plague the little nooks and crannies of the piece and interfere with its embossed areas. Wiping while the polish is still wet can save you a considerable amount of time. If the polish dries, leaving conspicuous white areas, the fastest remedy is to buff them out with a soft clean brush.

Ornate Objects

Certain items pose a few problems for the happy polisher. Some are too detailed to allow for a reasonable polishing effort. Others have felt on the bottom (e.g., candlesticks) or on the back (e.g., silver picture frames).

Provided the object is not too tarnished, the speediest remedy is to use a silver polishing cloth, which comes already impregnated with a polishing compound. It really works. Just grab hold of the object (presuming it is free of abrasive grit) and rub lightly. Goddard's makes an excellent one that costs around $5. As with any standard polish, if the object is intended for eating or drinking after being polished, it must first be washed. Otherwise the tea may taste mighty peculiar. For heavy tarnish, use silver polish instead.

Prevention

Happily, in spite of the various precautions one must observe about and around silver, there are a number of preventive steps you can take to minimize the time you will spend polishing it.

- Keep the silver behind glass. It will tarnish far more slowly than if exposed to the variety of airborne substances that hasten the process. If the silver is exposed to salty ocean air, it is especially in need of such protection. Make sure the piece was polished well, preferably using a tarnish-retarding formula (which really does work). William Meyer, a San Francisco antique silver dealer, has kept pieces behind glass for up to 1½ years without repolishing!

- Many foods are a serious threat to silver. Tarnish is accelerated by salt and eggs in particular, but also olives, salad dressings, vinegar, some meats, and many fruits. Many of these foods are either acidic or sulfurous in nature. If these foods are displayed or dispensed in silver, try to use a glass liner or at least rinse and clean the silver very soon after use.

- Sulfur is the great chemical enemy of silver. It is the single greatest cause of tarnish in most homes. Sulfur is given off by deteriorating rubber, so don't store silver grouped together with rubber bands. The damage may not be reparable. Purists also don't wear rubber gloves when cleaning silver. (So *that's* why butlers wear white gloves!) Chamois also gives off hydrogen sulfide, so don't store silver wrapped in it either.

- When storing silver, it's best to use antitarnish protection strips and cloth bags. They contain a chemical tarnish preventive that will neutralize the hydrogen sulfide in the air. The strips are rated for about a year, the cloth bags for several years. Both Goddard and Hagerty have a line of such products. Camphor blocks are another traditional way of deterring tarnish if you don't mind the smell. Don't store silver in plastic bags or plastic wrap—both of which can trap moisture that could damage the silver.

- If your silver candlesticks are plagued by dripping wax, and you don't have the time to remove it every time you use them, consider buying round glass drip-catching disks traditonally called bobeches [bo-BESH]. (Annoy the in-laws with *that* one!) They have a hole in the middle through which the candle is placed. The glass surfaces are much more easily cleaned than ornate silver candlesticks—for example, with a cloth soaked in hot water. Or you can pop a clean one on the candlestick in a second if company is coming. There are times when The Clean Team seriously considers giving a set of those to all its customers whose candlestick and candelabra problems have become ours instead. Candle shops or good hardware stores should carry them.

bobeche

- Other steps you can take to minimize candlewax on silver (or any other) candlesticks are: (a) Use pure beeswax candles. They drip far less than other candles, if at all. Get the solid kind (they're hard as blazes to find now), not the kind that looks like beeswax directly from the hive; (b) Keep the candles out of a draft, which makes the flame burn so rapidly that it can't burn off the wax in time to avoid drips; (c) If you are using thick candles, consider installing brass candle tips that are typically used in churches and synagogues. These little upside-down cups shelter the flame from drafts and enable the candle to burn slowly and evenly. Available from religious-goods dealers.

Brass and Copper

Other metals typically do not come in as ornate a form as silver, so polishing is usually a more straightforward affair. The first thing to check, of course, is whether or not the metal has been lacquered to prevent tarnish. If so, polishes are out of the question. Just spray with Red or Blue Juice and wipe with a cloth as needed. If the lacquer has begun to break down or has been rubbed off in areas, little patches or cracks of oxidation will begin to show up. Then it's time either to strip the lacquer off (with lacquer thinner) and begin to polish the piece regularly, or strip it and relacquer it yourself or have a metalsmith do it for you.

Brass and copper can be cleaned with specialty polishes or generalized metal polishes. If the polish you're using leaves a chalk residue, follow the steps outlined for silver polishing to get rid of it. If the polish (e.g., Twinkle) calls for the object to be rinsed under water after polishing, resist your impulse to use hot water because it will hasten retarnishing. For the same reason, wipe all pieces completely dry after rinsing.

If you have a copper-bottom pot or pan that is particularly charred with heavy carbon buildup, lay an ammonia-soaked rag on the area for 15 to 20 minutes and then scrub with a white pad and polish. Repeat as needed.

Aluminum

Aluminum is a particularly difficult metal to clean once it becomes pitted or discolored. It will not respond to specialized cleaners as silver, brass, and copper will. Your best strategy is preventive: Keep aluminum surfaces free of alkalis (like soap scum in the bathroom) and salts that will etch it over time. What Red Juice will not clean probably will not come up. Some metalworkers rub with a cloth soaked in vinegar. (Never use ammonia on aluminum.) You might also try rubbing the surface with a damp cloth dabbed in cream of tartar, which is the same product that is used to boil away deposits in aluminum cookware. Expect modest but satisfying results. If you are truly ambitious, you can try to buff the surface with a buffing wheel and jeweler's rouge.

13   PREVENTION

The fastest way to clean is not to have to clean at all. You already knew that. Here are a few ideas about eliminating the cleaning burden before it gets a chance to accumulate.

Floors

- Don't buy a white resilient floor. It shows all the dark dirt.

- Don't buy a black resilient floor. It shows all the light dirt *and* smudges.

- *Especially* don't buy a black-and-white resilient floor. It shows everything. The greatest challenge in a floor, it has been argued, is a black-and-white checkerboard tile floor.

- A smooth floor covering is much simpler to maintain than a textured one.

- Locate doormats everywhere. An amazing amount of dirt is transported in through doors on the soles of shoes. But don't place a rubber-backed mat on vinyl or asphalt floors or the floor may become discolored.

- Seriously consider leaving shoes at the doorstep—perhaps just in one or two rooms of the house, if you encounter too much resistance to the idea.

- Use as little floor finish as humanly possible.

- Seal the floor properly. It will save you a lot of grief later because dirt will not be ground into the flooring itself.

- If you are installing resilient floor coverings, cove the edge rather than butting the flooring against the wall at a 90° angle. A coved edge doesn't trap dirt and is much easier to mop.

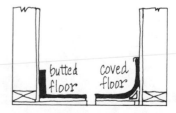

butted floor   coved floor

- Save a spare piece of carpet when you've had a new one installed. It will give you something to practice on when people like us annoyingly suggest that you try out a cleaning treatment on an "inconspicuous" piece of carpet. Moreover, if the carpet becomes permanently stained or otherwise damaged, it is often possible to patch in a new piece rather than replacing the entire carpet.

- Your choice of colors for the carpet can be critical. Solid dark and solid light colors are the most difficult to maintain. Tweed browns and grays are among the easiest.

- Most carpets sold these days are synthetic and have good resistance to staining. Nylon is an especially cleanable floor. Wool rugs are among the most beautiful, but enzyme cleaners and alkalis can attack wool fibers.

Kitchen

- Replace inefficient countertops if you can afford to. Grouted tile countertops can be beautiful, but they're lots of work to keep clean. If you have to keep them, seal the grout with a professional specialized sealer. If you can replace them, give some thought to a high-grade Formica or another durable surface. As in the case of floors, see if you can have a coved edge installed to prevent dirt building up in corners and edges. You will thank yourself every time you wipe the countertop.

- Remove baked-on spills in the oven by spraying the spot with Red Juice, scraping loose all that you can with your scraper, and removing anything left with a pumice stick. Very fast and simple. You can avoid using oven cleaner again for a long time.

Dust

- Consider investing in a real air filter—not just the tabletop variety. One of our clients was required to have an air filter on doctor's orders to help alleviate symptoms of emphysema. It ran 24 hours a day in the hallway about 10 feet from his front door. There wasn't a speck of dust three rooms away on the top shelf of the highest bookcase! He got it at Sears. In-line air filtration systems can also be installed in central air-conditioning and heating systems. Check with a contractor.

- Put small items behind glass.

Bathroom

- If the grout between the ceramic tiles is cracked or has shrunk or is powdering, it's time to regrout. Get a can of premixed grout from the hardware store and rub it into the cracks, following directions on the label. If the deterioration is serious and you have to remove all the grout, a specialized grout saw will speed the job along considerably. It's like a small hand-held hacksaw, except the 2-inch angled blade has a gritty carbide edge that cuts right through the grout at just the right width. It's worth its weight in grout.

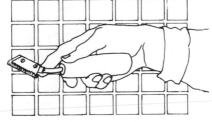

- After you've done such splendid work regrouting the tile, it would be a shame to let it go to seed again. *Do yourself a big favor.* Do what professional tile-setters do: *Seal the grout.* We recommend a penetrating sealer, which is usually in a base of mineral spirits. The surface sealers are often formulated with silicone, which can start to look like dried-on glue after a while and peel off. To help maintain the wonderful appearance of your fresh new grout, during your routine cleaning make sure you rinse it with particular thoroughness to neutralize any cleaning agents that might eat away at it over time.

- Put a squeegee in the shower and use it on the walls and especially on glass shower doors. It doesn't have to be a perfect job and you don't have to squeegee every square inch, but 30 seconds of squeegeeing after a shower adds up to lots of time saved. It makes scrubbing the tile easier and will make intervals between cleanings significantly longer. Naturally, the bathroom will also look much better between cleanings.

- Mineral deposits around faucets or outside the shower door can be caused by leaks or by pools of standing water. Repair the leaks by recaulking or replacing washers, and wipe up standing water as needed. You'll avoid ever having to remove that difficult mineral buildup again.

- Open the bathroom window so the mold doesn't flourish. If there isn't a window use a fan. Leave the bathroom door open (or ajar) when showering. Leave the bathroom door open whenever it's not in use, and spread out shower doors or curtains fully so they can dry.

- When the mood grabs you, you might want to take some Tile Juice and a white scrub pad into the shower with you . . . for the walls, not you. It's a fast way to do some quick touchups when company's on the way. Make sure you rinse thoroughly. If the buildup is heavy, don't try it because the floor of the tub or shower will get very slippery as the soap and mineral deposits are dislodged.

- Don't even think about installing a fiberglass shower enclosure. If it's already installed, replace it if you can afford to.

- If you have a persistent and otherwise unexplainable buildup of soap scum in your shower, it may just be the *soap*. Some of the bar soaps have a high fat content that will contribute to your cleaning burden. As an experiment, try different brands of soap—especially the newer liquid soaps—over a period of time. There are also totally fat-free, soap-free liquid skin cleansers like Cetaphil Lotion (Owen Laboratories). You may be amazed at the difference.

Light Bulbs

- Put a drop of light oil (WD-40, sewing machine oil, Vaseline, etc.) on the threaded base of a light bulb before you screw it in. This will prevent the bases from getting stuck when it's time to unscrew them. You know what a hassle it is when you twist the glass right off, leaving the base welded in the socket. Aluminum-based bulbs are especially vulnerable. If you have the choice, get bulbs with brass bases. They're far less likely to get stuck.

Silver

- Keep items under glass if possible. Keep them away from sulfur-generating things (e.g., rubber, many fruits, some oak furniture) and salt. Store in tarnish-resistant cloth if possible.

14   GETTING THE HOUSE READY FOR WEEKLY CLEANING

Ever since we told people in *Speed Cleaning* that our teams can clean a typical house in 42 minutes, we've received letters from readers about how to prepare a house *before* Speed Cleaning it. For example: "We've moved into a country home that I don't think has been cleaned in years. You wouldn't believe the amount of dirt and grime *everywhere*. I know I can't just take a feather duster to this mess!" Or: "A reasonable person wouldn't even try to clean the bathroom in our new apartment in the 12 minutes you talk about in *Speed Cleaning*. At this point it's beyond belief—or description."

Weekly Cleaning Versus Spring Cleaning

As usual, our highly intelligent readers are correct. Learning Speed Cleaning techniques and then whipping through your basically clean house in an hour or so on a weekly or biweekly basis can be very different from cleaning it the first time around. This is especially so if the house hasn't been really cleaned in some time. (Let's not dwell on the amount of time . . . or why.) The difference is that Speed Cleaning methods are for cleaning on an ongoing (maintenance) basis. But often a variety of tasks have to be accomplished before you can even begin to maintain a clean home. If you've been keeping a perfectly clean house or move into one, you can dive right into the time savings offered by Speed Cleaning without tackling the tasks in this chapter. If not, this chapter will help you get started.

Organization Problems?

There are homes in which a reasonable person wouldn't (couldn't) attempt maintenance cleaning, but the problem is more a matter of organization than cleaning. For example, in the kitchen the problem may not be a long-term collection of dirt, grime, and grease, but instead a fairly short-term collection of dirty pots and pans on the stove top and surrounding counters. And maybe there are dirty dishes from the last few days filling the sink and overflowing onto additional counter space . . . children's toys strewn about on the floor . . . a 75% complete jigsaw puzzle on additional counter space . . . and coats, clothes, and shoes on and around the chair in the corner. We're sure you could paint an even more complete picture.

Such a room needs to be picked up first, not cleaned first. There is a huge difference. You should fill the dishwasher—not haul out specialized cleaning tools. You should pick up the toys and clothes—not rent a floor machine. This is as much an organizational problem as it is a cleaning problem. (We would like to tackle that subject—but not in this book.)

You already really know what you have to do. Put things away before you start to clean. Threaten or cajole other family members to do so also. If you just put things away when you finish with them your life will be transformed. Hang up your coat when you take it off instead of first tossing it on a chair for a day or two. It's easier and faster, your house will look better, and the rooms won't be cluttered all the time. But you already knew that. Now all that remains is to do it. You may have a little fight with yourself when you do, but go ahead and be organized in spite of yourself. Fake it until it's routine enough to become a genuine impulse. Now let's get on to some of the cleaning tasks you may have to get out of the way to be able to begin the easier weekly (maintenance) cleaning.

In the rest of this chapter, we'll talk about situations where routine cleaning gets out of hand: The shelves are too dusty to use a feather duster; the shower-door tracks have devolved into miniature snake pits; the fiberglass tub no longer responds to anything you try. In the other chapters in this book, we tackle the more serious and independent spring-cleaning jobs step by step.

This chapter builds on the methods we discussed in *Speed Cleaning* for routine weekly cleaning, so for it to be most helpful it would be best if you were familiar with our earlier book. The chapter is designed to help you get through the first-time cleaning of an especially dirty house—without repeating all the instructions in *Speed Cleaning*. As in the case of Speed Cleaning, if you have any questions or problems on cleaning techniques please call or write us. We will be happy to give you our personal attention: 415-621-8444.

The Bathroom

If the entire room needs cleaning from top to bottom, start by washing the ceiling and then the walls (see Chapters 5 and 6). Don't worry about the mirrors or the sink or the toilet or shower right now. Don't even worry about covering such things up. Just let the drips and splashes fall where they may, unless the room is carpeted. (In which case you will need a drop cloth.) When you come to a light fixture (either over the sink or on the ceiling) put its glass bowl in the dishwasher unless it could be damaged. Most won't be, and the dishwasher cleans them very nicely. Remember, this is *not* routine Speed Cleaning. We wouldn't dream of hauling a light fixture off to the dishwasher during regular maintenance cleaning. We would just dust it, which takes a couple of seconds, and move on. Right now, we're as interested in smart cleaning as we are in fast cleaning. If the light fixtures themselves are old and rusty and an eyesore, throw them away and replace them. You don't have to be very handy to do this, and the fixtures are often inexpensive. The same is true for replacing glass bowls missing from the fixtures. Both of these steps can really enhance your spring-cleaning efforts.

After the ceiling and walls are out of the way, most of the rules of Speed Cleaning apply to a heavy-duty cleaning. It's just harder and more time-consuming. But taking the time to get the bathroom as clean as it will ever be will save you time in your maintenance cleaning all year long.

Use the toothbrush liberally since it will get into long-neglected dirty corners and other areas that are difficult to clean or reach. If you use it correctly you may wear out a couple of them the first time through. Fine—that's what they're for. Use them around the sinks and faucets, towel racks, switch plates, corners of mirrors, pictures, and anything else you come across. Spray with Red Juice, agitate with the toothbrush, and wipe with a cleaning cloth.

Shower Enclosure

When the shower is truly despicable, rely heavily on chemical cleaning power. That is, apply Tile Juice, wait (which means move on to something else to clean), and then scrub. You *must* have a tile brush to do this job properly. Rinse, reapply Tile Juice, wait again, and rescrub. You can use a razor and white pad to help remove heavy layers of soap and hard water from the glass shower door. Remember to keep the surface wet and the blade at a low angle. *And be careful!* Use the toothbrush in corners and on grout that you can't reach with the tile brush.

If the above methods don't work, shift to a pumice stick. Always use it on a surface wet with Tile Juice, Red Juice, or water. But keep it away from fiberglass or metal or plastic surfaces. *Be careful or you will damage the wall.* Test a spot on the wall first to be sure it's safe against scratches. The pumice stick requires very little pressure to work a minor miracle, so don't press hard.

The "black stuff" (or, less commonly, "red stuff") that people always complain about in bathrooms is generally mold. Most of it will be removed when cleaning the shower/tub area. What's left can be killed by spraying it with a little chlorine bleach. Just before you leave the bathroom after cleaning it, open a window and spray the bleach directly on any remaining mold. You can use it full strength or diluted up to 3 parts water per 1 part bleach. Chlorine bleach is a very powerful cleaning agent, and we are discussing its use only on areas like ceramic tile that will not lose their color when treated with bleach. Treat bleach with utmost caution. After spraying it, leave the bathroom and close the door to avoid the fumes. Return in 20 minutes to rinse it thoroughly. Don't spray metal fixtures or allow bleach to drip on them. Also, adjust the nozzle of the spray bottle so it squirts instead of sprays in a mist. This will help control the direction of application as well as minimize the amount of bleach vaporized into the air.

Shower-Door Tracks

It is a little-known fact that after God was finished creating hell, He had a few spare moments on His hands so He turned His attention to shower-door tracks—thus creating a little branch office of hell here on earth. It's hard to imagine how so much dirt, sludge, soap scum, mineral deposits, and grunge can accumulate so fast in so small a space.

Advance Preparation

If you are organized well enough, you can cut down your time on this job considerably if you vacuum the tracks *when they are bone dry*. Use the long-nosed vacuum attachment along with a dry toothbrush to loosen up the grunge. You will also be getting rid of most hair, which causes a significant management problem when you're cleaning, and especially rinsing.

Cleaning

This procedure is messy, but it works for especially filthy and neglected tracks. Spray them liberally with Red Juice and clean with the tile brush. This big brush gets into both tracks at the same time. It also splashes Red Juice and recently liberated grunge out of the tracks into the tub on one side, the floor on the other side, plus you. This needs to be done just once, so persevere. Besides, you haven't cleaned the floor or tub yet, anyway.

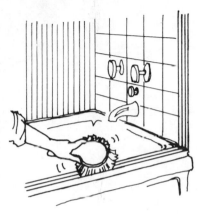

If necessary, shift to more heavy-duty tools in this order: After the tile brush, try the toothbrush for those last hard-to-reach spots. Then try the white pad folded to fit into the track, and then the scraper with a cleaning cloth around it. Twist the scraper so it is tight against both sides of the track.

Rinsing

It's much more laborious to rinse the tracks than to clean them. Drain holes in the base of the middle rail between the two tracks are designed to drain water from the outside track to the inside track and then to the tub itself. Trouble is, they cross-feed rinse water and grunge back and forth between the two tracks until you're ready to have fits. Blotting up the dirty solution with a sponge or even cleaning cloths takes forever.

(Tub side)

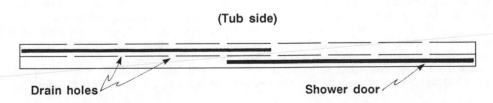

Drain holes   **Shower door**

It's fastest to rinse with a shower wand if you have one. This will cause water to splash all over, but it will wash the loose grunge into the tub if you keep at it. Any water on the floor is potentially damaging to the floor covering, so don't get carried away. If you don't have a shower wand, use a large container to pour water into the tracks. An outdoor watering can works very well. Pour lots of water so you're not really using all those drain holes that are probably clogged with grunge anyway. Instead, the water is running over the top of the tracks and carrying the grunge with it. Try to direct the water so more of it is running into the tub than onto the floor. This is easier said than done, however, so put down cleaning cloths or towels on the floor to catch the overflow as necessary.

Even rinsing as thoroughly as this, it is still difficult to stop grunge from moving back and forth and from side to side. Keep at it, and you'll get most of it. You may be able to strategically place a cleaning cloth in the tracks to help prevent backflow when rinsing. But don't even try to rinse away the very last of the grunge. Instead, use cleaning cloths to wipe out the last residue left over after rinsing. Resist the impulse to forbid anyone from ever using the shower again.

Recaulking

First a clarification of terms: We're using "caulk" to refer to the band of material that seals the junction between tile and the tub, or between the shower-door track and the tub, or other junctions where water might leak or collect. It's usually squeezed from a tube. We're using "grout" to refer to the plasterlike material between individual tiles that was rubbed in when the tile was installed. This section is about recaulking only. In Chapter 13, "Prevention," we say a few words about regrouting.

If the caulk is damaged or missing in areas around the tub, or if it has mold growing deeply in or behind it, take the time to repair it. If you don't correct this problem now, you will leave areas where moisture will be trapped and mold will flourish. Also, old caulk will continue to break loose when you scrub it. Repairing it will reduce your maintenance cleaning time all year long.

The time to get started on repairing the caulk is when you're cleaning the shower or tub area. Dig out the loose pieces of caulk. Or remove it all if you can. It's easier to replace it that way and it looks better when you're finished. Use the scraper from your apron pocket.

Clean out the areas where the caulk was removed. Use Red Juice and the toothbrush, and rinse thoroughly. Then finish cleaning the shower/tub. If there was any mold in the caulk, spray the entire area you're going to repair with chlorine bleach. Do this after you've finished cleaning the whole room and just prior to leaving the room. Return in 20 minutes to rinse the bleach residue. Then *let the area dry thoroughly.* Before anyone uses this shower again, recaulk.

Do the recaulking carefully. First, follow the manufacturer's directions to the letter. Do it their way. They want it to look nice so you'll buy more of their product. Besides, they are bound to have more experience than you. Second, we have a recommendation about recaulking. Do the first line of caulk on the least conspicuous place—for example, the seam between the shower door and the tub. It's almost impossible to see this line from outside the shower, so this is a great place to practice. If you're not recaulking this area, choose the next least visible line on which to start. The same is true for caulking around the sink or the base of the toilet, where these same techniques can also be applied. (We never said this was going to be easy—but it is rewarding.)

Fiberglass

We get more questions from people on how to clean fiberglass than any other surface. Fiberglass is one of those products that is far more popular with its installers than with

anyone who has to clean it. It is many times faster to install than grouted ceramic tile, but you'll notice that the installers don't stick around long enough to have to clean it, do they?

First, try not to neglect it. The reason we get all these questions is because it isn't easy to clean—so you are really compounding the problem if you let it go.

Manufacturers issue dire warnings not to use any sort of abrasive on fiberglass, and instead make utterly useless recommendations like using a mild liquid soap or detergent—which don't even faze a dirty fiberglass surface. Virtually every fiberglass cleaner on the market has abrasives, even though they may list them on the label as "earth minerals" or something else clever. There's nothing wrong with an abrasive as long as it's not too coarse and you don't rub too hard.

We've heard all sorts of suggestions for cleaning agents—ranging from fiberglass specialty products to the rubbing compound you use on your car. The two we're most satisfied with are Comet (the can swears it's now safe for use on fiberglass) and a Turtlewax product called Scratch Guard. Apply either with a cleaning cloth or white pad on smooth surfaces. For irregular surfaces, use the toothbrush or tile brush as well.

The most difficult cleaning problems involving fiberglass are to be found with floors that have very fine-grained strips designed to keep you from slipping. You can get these as clean as possible with your tile brush and Comet or Scratch Guard. (Because this finish is like sandpaper, you can't use white or green pads, steel wool, or cleaning cloths.)

To use the tile brush correctly (or any cleaning brush, for that matter), don't bear down as hard as you can to try to make it work better. You're only making things worse. That extra pressure splays the bristles to one side or the other, so they aren't really scrubbing anything—they're only rubbing the surface. This is a place where the "don't work harder, just smarter" concept is particularly true. Feel with the brush so that you are digging the individual tips of the bristles into the dirt lurking in the sandy, rough finish. If you do, you'll get results.

After you have cleaned the entire floor, if it still isn't as white as you'd like, try a little chlorine bleach. Open the window or door. Put a few layers of white paper towels on the shower floor and soak them with bleach. The paper towels keep the bleach from running directly into the drain. Toss the paper towels after half an hour or less (*carefully!*), rinse well, and your fiberglass is now as clean as it's going to get.

Hard-Water Deposits

The second-most-often-asked question we hear is how to remove mineral rings or hard-water deposits around toilets and sinks. A pumice stick is a great tool for removing such stains from areas it can reach. To avoid scratching the surface, use the pumice stick when the surface is wet. On a porcelain sink or toilet, Tile Juice is a useful wetting agent. Otherwise, use Red Juice or water.

One way to get rid of the deposits that accumulate around the sink faucets and outside of the shower doors is to use the razor to break the deposit loose from the porcelain. If the razor leaves black marks, remove them with Comet and a toothbrush or cloth. Unfortunately, the deposit will start building up again, but if you clean the area occasionally like this during your regular cleaning, it should never get thick again.

Plants—Hanging or Otherwise

For undeniably noble and sentimental reasons, more people seem to have a dusty, dirty, decidedly unhealthy plant hanging in the bathroom than in any other place in the house. Most of these plants are at least three-fourths dead, and you really can't see the leaves through the ¼-inch layer of dust on them. Do the plant a favor and toss it. It's not really a family member, and you will still be a decent human being if you make compost out of it. And your bathroom will be greatly improved. If you miss the plant, get another one. Just promise yourself that you will take care of it next time.

Then go through the house with the same benign ruthlessness toward any other plants that merit it. My own mother has a split-leaf philodendron that is older than I am. And it looks it. (Poor thing.) In the living room, yet!

Plants get just as dirty as anything else in a room. They need cleaning as well as watering. If you wash or dust or otherwise maintain your plants, you may not have to dispose of them in six months. Unfortunately, many people seem to treat plants the same way they treat Levolors (miniblinds)—by doing nothing. Sorry, in both cases you'll need to keep them clean as part of regular maintenance cleaning. You may not have to clean every inch of each plant or miniblind every time, but neither can you ignore them forever. The correct procedure is to do some of them each time you clean. Depending on the plant, a feather duster or a damp cloth is the instrument of choice.

The Kitchen

The same sequence applies to the kitchen as well as the bathroom: Clean the ceiling and walls first. Whether or not you wash the ceiling, put dirty light fixtures that you can safely remove, and that can stand it, into the dishwasher. Wash others by hand and replace. Clean the remaining part (the base) of the fixture when you come to it. If the track lights look terrible upon close inspection, clean them in place. Turn them off, let them cool, and spray and wipe with Red Juice. Resolve to try to remember to look up more often when you're cleaning and to dust them with the feather duster in the future.

Now clean the cabinet doors if they need it. This is also an appropriate time to clean out the cabinets, which you would do before cleaning the doors themselves.

Cabinets aren't easy to clean because they are usually neglected for many months.

There is usually a buildup of grease, fingerprints, and other dirt that has made its way through your home and gravitated toward the kitchen.

For wood cabinets, we use a "furniture feeder"—a solution of a solvent and other cleaning and restorative agents. It cleans well and leaves a coat of carnauba wax to protect the surface until it needs cleaning again. Apply the furniture feeder with an old (disposable) cleaning cloth. Use a second cloth to wipe it away before it dries. Use fine steel wool (0000), a white pad, or a toothbrush to help clean the cabinets. Use the toothbrush liberally if the wood has grooves or designs that you can't easily clean with the steel wool and a cloth. Clean the inside of the door first. If you're lucky, inside the cupboard door may only need a touchup for the inevitable fingerprints and spots here and there.

If the cabinets have a gloss or semigloss painted surface (it doeesn't matter whether it's wood or metal beneath), clean with the same clear ammonia solution you use on the walls (see Chapter 6, "Washing Walls") or use Red Juice in a spray bottle. These are much easier to clean than wood cabinets. Use your white pad and toothbrush on any problem areas.

The Stove

Another area that usually needs serious attention before you can attempt weekly cleaning of the kitchen is the *inside* surface of the stove. Beyond the pale of routine cleaning is the area under the top of your stove. Most stove surfaces just lift up after sliding them forward a bit. If you have the owner's manual, check it for instructions. If not, you might call the customer-service office of the manufacturer. Most have 800 numbers. (Call 1–800-555-1212 for directory information on 800 numbers.)

Under the stove top is one of those places to clean that illustrates your particular degree of compulsion. For instance, I barely care how much dirt and other grunge is accumulating there because I can't see it. However, I know people who practically lay

awake at night worrying about this kind of unseen dirt. If there is a problem with pests (or "visitors," as pest-control people delicately say), then you should keep this area clean regardless of how compulsive you are.

The way we clean this area is first to pick up any large pieces of debris (like dog biscuits or chopsticks) and then to vacuum it with the long-nosed plastic attachment. Don't use a brush attachment, as there is enough grease here to ruin it for future use. Use the long-nosed attachment in conjunction with your toothbrush. Agitate with the toothbrush while holding the vacuum attachment close by to inhale the debris as you loosen it. After I have done this I'm quite happy with the degree of cleanliness in this unseen area and I replace the top and move on. If it takes additional cleaning to satisfy your individual standards, use Red Juice, a cloth, and the toothbrush.

Earlier we mentioned one of the least favorite things to clean in the kitchen: a clogged kitchen filter in the stove's exhaust unit. Often it can become totally encrusted with hardened grease. It's important to keep it unobstructed or that grease will end up on the walls or ceiling. A clogged filter will also put an increased load on the fan motor. The fastest cleaning solution is to pop the filter in the dishwasher. It will do an amazing job. If the filter is beyond cleaning, it will console you to know that replacement filters are very reasonable. Buy two and keep one in reserve.

The Rest of the Kitchen

There usually isn't a lot of high dust in a kitchen. If so, and if it isn't greasy, and if you didn't wash the walls and ceilings already, make a trip around the room knocking it down. You can use a broom or the vacuum with a brush attachment. If the dust is impregnated with grease, don't knock it down. Either use the vacuum with no attachment to get the worst of it, or use the broom to catch it. But don't let it fall all over everything. Or you can keep cleaning normally and spray and wipe it off as you come to it.

The same techniques used in the bathroom with your toothbrush will help with difficult areas here in the kitchen. Hard-water problems are solved in the same way also, but don't use a pumice stick on a stainless-steel fixture.

Remember the poor plant in the bathroom? In the kitchen it has been reincarnated as a dirty, stained, misshapen sponge by the sink. Sometimes right next to it is a scrubber of some vintage that is barely recognizable as such anymore. Please throw them away. Ignore tips about how to rejuvenate or otherwise bring these poor things back to life. Bury them. Replace the sponge whenever the old one looks dirty or starts to stink. (I get them in packs of four for about 20 cents each.) Also replace the scrub brush, and then leave it under the sink instead of out with the sponge. They learn bad habits from each other.

When all these tasks are finished, you can start the normal/maintenance/routine Speed Cleaning trip around the kitchen. There is undoubtedly harder work to do during this initial cleaning, but routine Speed Cleaning won't go very fast until you're finished with this preliminary cleaning. Have an extra supply of Red Juice on hand, lots of cleaning cloths, and abundant perseverance.

The Dishwasher Rule

This rule applies to things found in any room of the house: *If it fits, put it in the dishwasher.* This includes: light fixtures from any room or the front or back porch; the grease filter over the stove; many porcelain knickknacks that get filthy over time; any removable parts of the can opener, toaster oven, or other small appliances; some dish-drying racks; or any other items that you can think of that would not be affected by the hot water, detergent action, and heat of drying. The welfare of some of these items will require that you skip the dishwasher's extremely hot drying cycle. You may be amazed at how sparkling clean the dishwasher can get items that had caked-on dust or grease—especially ones with lots of little nooks and crannies that are murder to get at any other way.

The Rest of the House

Now that the "wet" jobs are out of the way, it's downhill from here. The biggest chore left before you can begin weekly cleaning is probably lots of vacuuming. Our general rule is to vacuum almost everything first if there is a heavy buildup of dust. Even if you're going to wash the woodwork or the windows, you should vacuum the woodwork and sills first to avoid having to remove all the mud you'd make. The vacuum will quickly remove the dust in the corners and on the small bits of the woodwork. If you get that same dust wet, it's far more difficult to wipe it out of all the corners and tight spots.

Heavy Dust

Before we go on about dust per se, indulge us in a short rumination. We were astounded one day when somebody asked us what dust *is*. (Think about it. What is it, really—baby dirt? Will each piece of dust grow up to be a dirt clod?) Considering the fact that The Clean Team has collectively spent thousands of hours dealing with it, we really didn't have a ready response.

So we looked up *dust* in, naturally enough, the dictionary. We thought you might appreciate this remarkable definition from the *American Heritage Dictionary*. Starts out conventional and then gets pretty weird.

dust (dust) *n.*

1. Fine particulate matter.
2. A cloud of such matter.
3. Such matter regarded as the result of disintegration.
4. Disturbance; confusion; excitement.
5. a. Earth, especially when regarded as the substance of the grave: "Dust thou art, and shalt to dust return." (Milton).
6. A debased or despised condition.
7. Something of no worth.
8. *British.* Ashes, household dirt, or rubbish. [From the Indo-European *dheu-*: The base of a wide variety of derivatives meaning "to rise in a cloud," as dust, vapor, or smoke, and related to semantic notions of breath, various color adjectives, and *forms denoting defective perception of wits.* (Emphasis added.)]

Disintegration! Confusion! Debasement! Defective wits! All that having to do with lowly dust . . . who would have imagined?

But back to the practical side of the subject at hand. Routine dust management is a task for daily or weekly cleaning. As we discussed in *Speed Cleaning*, your main ally in the war against dust is a professional feather duster made of ostrich down.

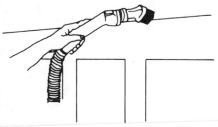

But what do you do if you encounter a really nasty accumulation of dust—something beyond the capacity of a feather duster? Something like, let's say, under the refrigerator, in a storage room, or in back of the washer/dryer, or behind Aunt Sophie's hatbox collection in the closet? In such cases, the feather duster would not be able to absorb the volume of dust and would just spread it around.

The main objective, besides removing dust, is not to make work for yourself by spreading the dust into the air or onto other surfaces. There is a difference between "old dust" and "new dust": Old dust is the dust you are trying to remove. New dust is what will resettle two minutes after you finish cleaning. Keep *new* dust to a minimum by making as little as possible of the *old* dust airborne. This is best done during heavy cleaning by using the vaccum cleaner rather than the feather duster. The equipment of first choice is the Little Vac equipped with the long-haired brush attachment at the end of the hose.

Vacuuming

If there are very dusty rafters, ceilings, or heavy cobwebs in your home, you should make an initial trip around the room with a long vacuum wand or broom to speed up the job. It's surprisingly easy to crash into things while you're doing that, so be extra careful.

The way to vacuum heavy dust is to start in one corner of the room and work your way around the perimeter of the room. Start high to get the cobwebs and high molding, and then vacuum all the way to the floor molding. Be sure to vacuum pictures and small objects as you come to them. Carefully.

If the objects are densely spaced in an area, you'll have to vacuum one, put it down in a clean spot, and repeat these steps for all other objects in the immediate area. Place each object in the temporary area in the same relative position in which you had originally found it so it will be easier to restore everything to the original positions. Then vacuum the shelf or area in which the objects were originally located and restore the objects to their original positions.

Also vacuum lampshades, mirrors, furniture, plants (as is possible, or shake them thoroughly), drapes, miniblinds, window frames and sills, shelves, shutters, and heater and exhaust vents. Make a special effort around the TV, VCR, and stereo—especially their power cords. Vacuum the TV knobs and the cloth over the speakers. Move the TV out from the wall if you can manage it or if you can find some help. Vacuum the back thoroughly and the floor area where it was. In fact, move anything and everything in the room that you can when doing heavy cleaning. In the middle of the room, vacuum the furniture and light fixtures (including their chains). As with the other rooms, clean light fixtures in the dishwasher if possible. If the fixture has been broken for months, now is the time to get serious about replacing it. It's not fair to spend a day or two making your home sparkle and then have company notice mainly the broken fixture in the hallway.

Use a 50-foot extension cord when vacuuming so you don't waste time having to stop to unplug and replug it all the time. You can't imagine how much time this will save until you've tried it.

The vacuum may need your help under these heavy dust conditions. If you encounter large debris that may clog the vacuum, pick it up and pop it into the debris pocket of the cleaning apron. The vacuum doesn't like things like straw, string, or thread, even though they don't appear to clog the hose. They act as a trap for debris in the vacuum hose and can build up to a genuine clog in no time at all. So resist the temptation to inhale such things into the vacuum.

Check the vacuum bag. Please. Don't go through the effort of vacuuming the entire house without checking to see if the bag is full! It's a false economy to be too frugal with vacuum bags: Don't wait until the bag is bulging at the seams before you change it. A stuffed bag puts a significant load on the vacuum motor and interferes with its ability to clean. Some professionals change it when it's only half full.

While you're using the vacuum, pay attention to the noise of the motor. If it shifts to a high whine, stop and check the bag. If the bag isn't full, there's a clog in either the hose or the wand. To find out where it is, disconnect the hose or sections of wand at various intervals and put your hand over the end. If putting your hand over the end does not make any difference—that is, the vacuum continues to be clogged and you feel no suction—then the clog is downstream: somewhere between your hand and the bag. If the motor suddenly jumped back down to its normal pitch when you disconnected the hose—that is, putting your hand over the end made the motor whine again and you felt suction—then the clog is upstream: somewhere between the inlet and where you separated the wand. This sounds more complicated than it is in practice: It's just a matter of locating the clog, which is worth the effort. We're amazed when

people vacuum an entire house with a full vacuum bag or clogged hose. It's hard enough to vacuum once, let alone having to do it all over again and have it be an exercise in futility! Most clogs can be cleared by reversing the direction of suction.

If you have a model with a motorized beater-bar attachment, one other mechanical thing you might check is the condition of the fan belt. Once again, some people are content to vacuum the whole house with the beater bar inoperative. It may be due to a burned-out motor or bad connection of the power cord, but the most likely cause is a fan belt that has hopped off its tracks or snapped apart. If the problem recurs regularly, the suction of the beater bar on the surface of the rug may be too great and the fan belt may be put under too great a strain as a result. If so, reduce the suction with your particular machine's way of compensating—usually an adjustable opening to let more air in the wand. To replace the fan belt, be brave. Flip the beater bar on its back and remove the backplate with a screwdriver. The rest is just common sense. If all else fails, read the directions.

Chandeliers

A chandelier is one thing you do *not* want to take apart and pop into the dishwasher. There are several specialized chandelier cleaners on the market that allow you to clean them in place.

Whichever product you decide to use, it's just a matter of inundating the chandelier with the sprayed-on solution from top to bottom. Then let it drip-dry onto a layer of newspapers you've placed under it. A sensible precaution is to lay down a piece of plastic or an old sheet underneath the newspapers. The newspapers can become saturated and transfer ink to the carpet.

Before you spray the chandelier, vacuum or dust it if possible. Obviously, you must turn the chandelier off and let it cool before you spray it. Because of this, you may have to bring supplemental lighting into the room to see what you're doing.

Spray liberally. Aim straight at the chandelier or from slightly below it, but not from above. This will minimize the amount of liquid that soaks into the light sockets. As you spray, you will notice that a coat of dirt comes loose almost immediately and starts dripping onto the newspapers below. Continue spraying each area until the visible dirt has been rinsed off and clear solution is all you can see on the chandelier. You can approach the individual pieces from countless angles. Try to follow as many of them as possible while spraying. After you've sprayed it, you can enhance your cleaning job by wiping dry the pieces of crystal that are easy to reach and can be wiped safely—both for you and for the chandelier.

Before cleaning any type of light fixture, make sure the bulbs are not only extinguished but are cool as well. When a bulb is hot, the filament is as frail as a piece of cigarette ash. One little jiggle and the filament will be destroyed. Also a hot bulb may explode if you spray it with a cool liquid cleaner.

Minor Repairs

My kitchen wall has a gouge in the door frame that was created when I dropped the lid of a pot. (No, I don't know how it hit the door frame before it hit the floor.) It is an ugly, dark, very visible scar in the otherwise clean white woodwork. If you're spring cleaning and you come across something similar in your own home, think about patching it with spackle and spot-painting it as a follow-up to the cleaning job. This minor repair process may not be the same caliber as a professional would do. You may even redo it when you get around to painting the room. But for now, even if the spot looks a little different from the rest of the wall (cleaner, or shinier, or whatever), the overall effect is quite positive. A spot that once bothered you practically every time you walked into the room will have disappeared.

Other simple repairs can make a big impact on the appearance of a room. Is one of the plastic electrical switch or outlet plates broken or missing? Have you wished they were all white instead of three different colors? Before you go to the store to get the spackle, count how many of each type of cover you need and pick them up also. These items are often less than 50 cents apiece. The cumulative effect of a small repair or two, changing all the switch plates to one color, and thoroughly cleaning the room can be quite gratifying.

Take a look around the house. Notice the things that bother you. You'll be surprised how many of those things can be corrected by cleaning them, easily repairing them, inexpensively replacing them, or simply tossing them. Good luck!

Maintenance

Now that the house is clean, you can start Speed Cleaning on a regular basis. There is nothing left in the way to stop you from saving all the time that's possible. It's amazing how housecleaning can be reduced to such a short period of time using today's techniques rather than the full-time methods passed down from our grandmothers.

APPENDIX:
HOW TO ORDER TOOLS, EQUIPMENT,
AND SUPPLIES

In the 12 months after *Speed Cleaning* was released, we received well over 10,000 requests from readers for more information about the actual products we use. It made little sense to write about a cleaning method if we didn't offer some way of enabling you to find the products we mentioned.

Because we use cleaning products daily and test new ones continuously, we have developed very definite opinions about them. We know what works and won't tolerate anything that doesn't. Some of the products have a higher initial cost, but they last two or three times longer than the cheaper alternatives. Others have replaceable parts that save money in the long run. And others cost more but just plain work better. For example, even if those cheap chicken feather dusters were free, we still wouldn't use them because they don't work. We much prefer to pay a fair price for ostrich-down feather dusters that work and that save us time week after week. And if something new comes along that works better, we change products. We aren't committed to any brand name or manufacturer—only to excellence.

One way to save time in your own housecleaning is not to have to endure all the tests and trials of products that we do. But even if you know what products you want to use, it still takes time to purchase them—especially if they're not carried at the local grocery or hardware store, which is true of many of the professional products we use. Our catalog can save you time on both accounts, because you can make your choices without leaving your home.

The *only* products we offer are the same ones we actually use in the field all day long. There's only one heavy-duty liquid cleaner, for example, because that's the best one we've ever found. And we've been looking for 10 years!

If you would like a free copy of our catalog please write us at:

The Clean Team
2264 Market Street
San Francisco, CA 94114

If you're in a hurry, call us at 415-621-8444 and we'll mail you one the same day.

BIBLIOGRAPHY

American Institute of Maintenance. *Carpet Selection and Care*, 3rd ed. Glendale, CA: American Institute of Maintenance, 1982.

Brandt, Herb. *How to Remove Spots and Stains*. New York: Putnam, 1987.

Bigelow-Sanford, Inc. "Commercial Carpet Maintenance Guide." Bigelow-Sanford, Box 3089, Greenville, SC 29602.

Feldman, Edwin B. *Supervisor's Guide to Custodial and Building Maintenance Operations*. Irvine, CA: Harris Communications, 1982.

Garstein, A. S. *The How-to Handbook of Carpets*. Monsey, NY: The Carpet Training Institute, 1979.

Massey, Frederick R. *The Professional Window Cleaning Manual*. Valley Center, CA: MBM Books, 1983.

Readers Digest Association, Inc. *Readers Digest Do-It-Yourself Manual*. Pleasantville, NY: Readers Digest, 1977.

Sack, Thomas F. *A Complete Guide to Building and Plant Maintenance*, 2nd ed. Englewood Cliffs, NJ: Prentice Hall, 1963.

Sandwith, Hermione, and Stainton, Sheila. *The National Trust Manual of Housekeeping*. Harmondsworth, England: Penguin Books, 1984.

Shrode, Terry. "Installing a Sheet-vinyl Floor," *Fine Homebuilding* (August/September 1984): 44–49.

Wright, Veva Penick. *Pamper Your Possessions*, rev. ed. Barre, MA: Barre Publishing, 1979.